# CRAPS
## A SMART
## SHOOTER'S
## GUIDE

# CRAPS
## A SMART SHOOTER'S GUIDE

# THOMAS MIDGLEY

**GBC PRESS**
P. O. Box 98115
Las Vegas, NV 89193
www.gamblersbookclub.com

GBC Press books are published by Gambler's Books Club in Las Vegas, Nevada. Since 1964, the legendary GBC has been the reigning authority on gambling publications and the only dedicated gambling bookstore anywhere.

Library of Congress Catalog Number: 2011925831
ISBN 10: 1-58042-282-9    ISBN 13: 978-1-58042-282-6
GBC Press is an imprint of Cardoza Publishing

## GBC PRESS
### c/o Cardoza Publishing
P.O. Box 98115, Las Vegas, NV 89193
Toll-Free Phone (800)522-1777
email: info@gamblersbookclub.com
### www.gamblersbookclub.com

## About the Author

Thomas Midgley, an engineer who graduated from Cornell University, rolled his first natural in a home craps game when he was only five years old, beating his father out of a few dollars. He later used his mathematical training and love for the game to analyze how dice perform. He found out that the dice operate in cycles—and discovered why most systems players lose.

Midgley did not use computer simulations to generate his statistics. He got his data in real games with live players, standing alongside other players at noisy crap tables. He painstakingly and accurately recorded 7,500 rolls of the dice while shooting craps at five landmark casinos in Las Vegas. Combining deep analysis of the data with mathematical investigations of crap odds, probabilities, and return ratios, Midgley formulated the powerful ideas in this book.

*This book is dedicated to my friend Gus Poulsen, with whom I have crawled on the floors of the casinos in Las Vegas hoping to find a friendly nickel, dime, or a discarded gambling chip with which we could start to rebuild our lost fortunes.*

# *T* TABLE OF CONTENTS

# FOREWORD

### By GBC Editors

You're holding in your hands a book that will change the way you look at craps. More importantly, it will change your results.

Hot and cold streaks form the basis of every serious crap player's belief—and often their strategy. This is the only book that *mathematically* shows you how take advantage of the cycles and patterns of dice and walk away with profit. Midgley has done all the research for you. He tells you exactly what to expect and exactly how to profit from dice cycles—rather than losing your money making bad bets with long odds.

If you can detect dice cycles and patterns, you'll have the secret to beating the game of craps. No longer do you need to work on hunches or feel, or try to guess when hot streaks and cold streaks will happen.

*Craps: A Smart Shooter's Guide* shows you a scientific and mathematically proven way to determine what the dice are doing—and how to take advantage of their cycles. Everything you'll learn in this book has been tested in real games with live players. Midgley spent forty hours at five landmark casinos in Las Vegas and recorded 7,500 actual rolls of the dice to give you live casino results that he painstakingly and accurately recorded.

You get real information here, not barebones computer simulations, so that you can actually see and feel what happens

in real dice games. You'll learn how to make all the bets, understand how and when to place odds bets to your advantage, and you'll understand the math behind the probabilities of the game. Plus, you'll learn how to stop making the key mistakes that cause so many players to lose.

This book is about winning, making money at the dice tables. Using the results of Midgley's 7,500 rolls of the dice, you'll learn how reality can differ from theory—and how to increase your chances of making a profit at craps.

# 1 INTRODUCTION

Every year millions of tourists who visit Las Vegas try their hand at craps. With no knowledge of the inner workings of the game, most of them lose—even experts find it difficult to overcome the built-in house advantage. In fact, all experts in statistics and probability agree that it is impossible to win in any negative expectation situation. But while experts talk about infinity, what crapshooters care about most is the next 15 minutes! In this infinite game, there are patterns and cycles that you can use to great advantage as a crapshooter—provided you can detect which cycle the dice are in.

Although no money management method has been developed to completely overcome the house edge at craps, the study of dice cycles could be the answer for crapshooters who have enough patience and perseverance to use this knowledge to gain an advantage over the house.

If you're smarter than those uneducated moths that get trapped by the bright lights of get-rich systems and foolish gambles, you will reap great benefits from this book.

I show you what can be expected with craps. You will see a comparison of what should have happened during my 40 hours at the crap table with what actually occurred. More importantly, you will learn how the game should be approached in order to produce the best opportunities for winning. I do this by comparing theory to actual results as demonstrated by the 7,500 rolls of real data I compiled at dice tables under actual casino conditions in Las Vegas.

You will recognize the many mistakes that you've been making with your bets. In addition, you will learn sound reasons why you should approach the game of craps with a different philosophy than what you've used in the past.

The information in this book is designed to help you become more successful than in the past. I hope it will encourage you to develop new betting techniques and avoid making foolish bets that account for most of your large losses. I also hope to make you a winner at craps!

# 2 FIGURING OUT A WINNING STRATEGY

This book had its beginning in 1920 when as a six-year-old boy I bought a pair of ivory-colored, celluloid dice for fifty cents at Shellhaus Drug Store on Salem Avenue in Dayton, Ohio. I took the dice home and began playing with them. When my father observed what I was doing, he asked me if I knew how to play craps. When I shook my head no, he said, "If you have some money, I'll teach you." I had seven cents, and so the game began with a one-cent roll. Some time later my mother came into the room. I had won $1.85.

"You're not going to let him keep that?" she asked my father.

"I would have kept his seven cents if I could have won them," he replied.

I learned two basic lessons about the game of craps—first, that it was an easy way to make money, and secondly, a crap player should never complain about losing because he, too, would have kept the other fellow's money if he had won. Over the years I engaged in many crap games and developed a system of betting and fading bets that proved very successful. Then came college and my first introduction to a crap table at the XYZ Club in Ithaca, New York. The table allowed many new bets and made it possible for me to have action on every roll, which was much different than in private games. It also permitted me to bet any amount I wanted to wager.

The rest of this story is the same as that of every other crap-table addict: The more sophisticated my betting became, the larger the amount of dollar ammunition I required. And even though my short bursts of wins were large, my subsequent losses were much larger. One night I shifted my concentration and interest away from the dice, and began to study other players at the table. They were replicas of me! They won in bursts, but later lost their winnings plus a little more within a few hands.

One particular player came to a table one night, signed a pit check for $500, hit a run of luck, and within a few minutes had a $4,000 profit. He cashed out, and received nine of his former $500 checks, which he tore to pieces. I had been observing this performance and wondered how many other $500 checks this loser had outstanding in the pit. A short time later he returned, signed another $500 check, lost it all within minutes, swore, and left the table. There were many others like this addict, walking from table to table, searching for a winning streak.

There had to be a better way. I determined right there and then to figure out the best way to beat the game of craps. Soon after, I began my studies. The thought began to burrow into my consciousness that there must be more to the game of craps than the simple odds created by the 36 possible combinations of the dice.

I searched for books. What I found was disappointing. No one had gone any deeper into the game than the simple fundamental odds relationships that I could easily compute in my head. And yet, the authors of these books dwelled on these simple relationships as though they were delivering some profound dissertation on some new discovery that only they were privy to.

I would have to do the work from scratch myself.

I sat down and computed odds for all the bets offered on the crap table, plus odds for consecutive wins with these various bets. There were no great surprises. Everything favored the house. The next question was whether the dice ran in cycles. Were there times when some type of bet would be favored over the others? I realized that the only way to find out was to actually collect crap table data in a live game.

First, I attempted to record data while standing behind players at a table. This failed because unless I could see the dice, I could not record the roll accurately. I soon realized that standing at the table was the key to clear observation, and that I had to play to gain that position. It was a frightening prospect. I had demonstrated many times that I was capable of losing the "family fortune" in a matter of a few minutes at a crap table. A large number of hours at a crap table would certainly result in disaster, I feared.

Again it was back to the drawing board and reexamination of the basic odds. I developed a simple plan for betting. With a great deal of apprehension, I approached a table at the Frontier Hotel in Las Vegas where I bet the minimum $2. Five hours later I had a $30 profit. I could have lost $30 but it would have mattered little since I had accomplished my goal—I now had complete data on every dice roll, data that I would gladly have spent $30 for.

The next night I went to the Hilton Hotel, limiting myself to its $1 minimum bet, collecting another five hours of data— and $21 profit.

I took my 10 hours of data home and studied it. There were no surprises, but it appeared that a five-hour cycle was developing. To study my cycling theory, I returned to Las Vegas, this time spending 10 straight hours at a table in Caesars, 10 straight hours at a table in the Sands, and another 10 hours at a table in the Nugget. Combined with five hours of data from the Frontier and five hours of data from the Hilton, I had 40 total hours of crap table data with which to complete my studies. I also had another three winning sessions of $16, $22, and $47.

I now had ample data with which I could compare my theory. These comparisons gave me an understanding of how to play the game of craps more intelligently.

This book presents my conclusions on how you can best "defend" yourself in craps. It also explains the reasoning behind the conclusions. The book's purpose is to give you an arsenal of weapons for defending yourself against negative temptations and to show you how to place bets when your chances for success are best.

# 3 UNDERSTANDING THE CASINO'S ADVANTAGE

When Willie Sutton, the bank robber, was asked why he robbed banks rather than robbing some other entity, he said he chose banks because, "That was where the money was."

This same philosophy can be applied to gambling casinos. A person enters a gambling casino because he believes the easy money is there. Gambling casinos are there because owners expect people will leave casinos with less money in their pockets than when they arrived. Because casino owners are correct in judging how foolish people are with money, casinos grow larger, in size and number.

Although extracting some very large "wins" from the banks, Sutton wound up a loser, spending much of his life in prison. These prison confinements led to his second avocation—that of a famous escape artist. Career-wise, Sutton followed a repetitious routine. Bank robberies were followed by arrests that were then followed by confinements in penitentiaries, from which he escaped so he could rob more banks and be able to spend more time in more prisons.

Most gamblers follow a similar pattern. Each large loss is followed by confinement in regret. But when new bankrolls are acquired, they escape from their regrets and sally forth trying once more to court Lady Luck, only to be jilted again by her.

A crap player fancies that his every bet will be a winner. He defies odds and probabilities, repeating his mistakes over and

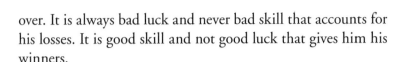
over. It is always bad luck and never bad skill that accounts for his losses. It is good skill and not good luck that gives him his winners.

# HOW HOPE IS A
# PLAYER'S DOWNFALL

Every crapshooter has watched other shooters roll the dice eighteen or twenty times before making a point. He has seen other rollers throw three or four consecutive 7's, roll five or six straight passes, and do all sorts of successful things. And each time he has witnessed the other fellow do one of these things he has told himself, "If he can do that, so can I." And every crap player has seen times when he too has made his point after eighteen or twenty rolls of the dice. On occasion, he has thrown three or four consecutive 7's. And each time he gets the dice, he tells himself, "If I could do it once, I can do it again."

These statements are true. If one person has done something with the dice, another person can produce the same results throwing the dice on a future throw. If it happened once, why not again?

The real question is: *When* will it happen?

If we could determine *when*, there would be no problem in winning. These things will always occur at some time, because long rolls and consecutive passes must take place occasionally if the game of craps is to have any relationship to the true mathematical probabilities of the game.

# PREYING OFF THE PLAYER'S WEAKNESSES

Every crap addict has winning fantasies. He imagines them while traveling to Las Vegas, Indian reservations, Atlantic City or wherever he plays his games. He conceives many while just standing at the crap table. Failure never sobers the crap lover's optimism. It may dampen his enthusiasm momentarily, but not to the extent where his hopes cannot be fully revived by new folding money for new chips. Only when his wallet is empty and his casino credit frozen does the sad realization of defeat burst his bubble of daydreams.

But this depression is short-lived. After a night of reflecting on his most recent mistakes, each new day brings new fantasies based on new betting schemes which, when mixed with fresh money in his wallet, completely restores self-confidence and zeal. He will once again march forth to do combat with the crap table on the floor of the casino's battlefield.

By definition, an expert is a "mechanic away from home." Each person standing around a crap table is an "expert," whether a bettor or a houseman. The stickman, the dealers, and referees work for the casino. They spend hours watching the antics of the dice. As a consequence, their words are heeded as the ultimate authority. How often have we been encouraged after hearing the stickman utter his sage question of "After craps, what?" to double the size of the bet we had just lost? Quite often a 7 will follow a crap, but not because of some magic attraction that 7's have for following craps. There are simply more combinations on the dice that produce 7's than any other number.

Housemen are experts, though not experts in the sense that they know more about winning than their customers. They are experts at selling various bets on the table and encouraging a double-size bet with their advertisements of "attractive" wagers.

Let your money receive a point of 4 or 10 on a come bet, and a houseman asks "Odds?" in a polite, persuasive way that leads you to feel that putting odds on your bet is the expert thing to do.

If a 2 is rolled, what do we hear? "Two. Craps. Don't come and double in the field!"

In such subtle ways, we are constantly reminded that there are bets available on the crap table other than pass—and that we have just lost the chance to pick up easy money by not having bet them. We are also hammered with many other reminders:

"Nine. Pay the come and field bets."

"Seven-out. Pay the last come, don't pass, and don't come. "

"New shooter coming out. Get your bets down! Who wants 11 and craps?"

Casino men are experts at advertising their wares, but take them away from their positions of supervising the table, place them around a crap table as bettors, and they will fare no better than any other bettor. They too become "mechanics away from home."

Each slot machine addict has its own way of pulling the handle. Some pull it fast, while others start slowly and end with a fast jerk. Some keep it slow all the way. The old models of slot machines are mechanical devices. It makes no difference how the arm is pulled or whether a man, woman, child, or monkey pulls it—the result will be the same. But the slot machine addict fantasizes that how he pulls the handle is very important. (Of course, pushing buttons in a particular manner on the newer breed of slot machines is equivalent to the techniques of slot handling in the old ones.)

Each crapshooter has his own way of throwing the dice. Some throw them high. Some throw them hard so that they bounce far back from the end of the table. Some shooters are dainty. Some rattle dice with long shakes before throwing them. Some people make a series of little rolls on the table in front of them so as to fantasize fending off a losing roll before throwing dice down the table. Some rub dice on the table, much the same as a bull pawing the dirt in the bullring before a charge. Like the bull in the ring, rubbing the dice's feet on the table will not prevent the eventual death of the hand.

It really makes no difference what antics a crapshooter displays when shooting dice. It makes no difference whether the dice are thrown by a man, woman, child, a left-handed monkey, or whether they are shot down the table from a mechanical device. Results will be the same. Why? Because, if these shooting antics really gave the shooter any advantage, every shooter could be a winner—and casinos would go broke.

# TURNING THE GAME AROUND TO YOUR ADVANTAGE

After reading these introductory chapters on craps, the next logical step to take in the pursuit of understanding and mastering the game is to dig deeper into the odds and probabilities of craps—the fastest, most exciting gamble on the casino floor.

# 4 THE DICE AND THEIR ODDS

A pair of dice is made up of two dies. Each die is a cube with each side of the cube marked with a different number of dots, numbering from one dot to six dots. If the sides of the die were to be marked with the numerals 1 through 6 instead of the dots, it would make no difference in the results of the games that are played with dice, but by using dots instead of numerals, the dice become universal as the dots have the same meaning in all languages. Forms of dice were in use long before many of our modern languages were developed.

A pair of dice is made up of two dies identical in size, color, and in the positions of their markings. It would make no difference to the results of dice games if the two dies were different in size or in color or in the relative positions of their markings. As long as each die was a perfect cube and had a different number, 1 through 6, represented on each of its six sides, the two cubes would function, in relation to each other, the same as though they were identical cubes. However, different sizes, colors, and markings would produce accusations of loaded dice.

Loaded dice are dice that have weighted sides in order to favor the production of certain numbers. Usually loaded dice are opaque (commonly ivory) with rounded corners making it easier for dies to be positioned by their weighted sides. Loaded dice often make appearances in the private games where some sharp crook fleeces the innocents. The players in a casino could adjust their betting to take advantage of the "loaded" positions so that loaded dice could act to the disadvantage of the house. There are many other forms of crooked dice.

Dice used in casinos have sharp corners. They are transparent, precisely balanced so that no one side is favored, and are marked in the conventional manner. If the face toward the observer is 5, the top of the cube will be 6, and the vertical face to the right will be 3. The face on the opposite side from 5 will be 2. The opposite face to 6 will be 1, and the face opposite to 3 will be 4.

If one of the dies was marked conventionally and the other was marked in any other way such as having a 2 on the opposite side of 6 (instead of one), a 4 on the opposite side of 5 (instead of 2), and a one on the opposite side of 3 (instead of 4), the odds of the game of craps would not be changed. But, the "intelligent" remarks and bets that the conventional dice markings promote would be lost, and the crap addicts would become less "expert."

## UNDERSTANDING THE DICE

One of the first things that a crapshooter learns is what the number is on the bottom of the dice, out of sight, resting on the table surface. For example, if a 7 is on the top of the dice, an identical 7 is on the bottom of the dice. Opposite each 7 made up of a 6 and a 1 is a 7 made up of a 1 and a 6. Opposite each 7 made up of a 3 and a 4 is a 7 made up of a 4 and a 3. Opposite each 7 made up of a 5 and a 2 is a 7 made up of a 2 and a 5.

Seven is the only number that has its same number appear on the opposite side. All the other numbers have supplementary numbers on their opposite sides. On any one die, the opposite sides add to 7. On a pair of dice, the opposite sides add to 14. This is why the opposite sides of all 7's are always 7.

Since the opposite of a 1 on a die is a 6, the opposite sides of a pair of dice showing 2 must be 12 (two 6's), and the total of the two sides is 14. On the opposite side of two dice adding up to 3 is 11. On the opposite sides of all combinations of two dice adding up to 4 are 10's. On the opposite sides of all combinations of two dice adding up to 5 are 9's, and on the opposite sides of all combinations of two dice adding up to 6 are 8's.

These things the new crap player learns early, and soon he is calling for the dice shooter to "turn them over" when the shooter rolls a number that is supplementary to the one he wants. This is basically trivia, but to the serious crap addict it has an importance he has fantasized, a fantasy that often will cause him to make a place bet on the number that is supplementary to the one rolled to pass.

# DICE EXPECTATIONS

If a person takes a penny and flips it into the air 100 or so times, letting it fall to the ground each time, regardless of how many times he starts with a head or a tail in the upper position he will have a final result close to 50 heads and 50 tails, which are the correct 50/50 odds for a flat coin that has two differently marked sides. Likewise, if a single die is rolled for a large number of times, the final result should show the same number of 1's, 2's, 3's, 4's, 5's, and 6's. This is also true whether two dice are rolled or six dice are rolled at each roll.

During the 40 hours that data was recorded, the dice were thrown 7,654 times, making 15,308 rolls of an individual die. The following tabulation shows the number of times that each die number appeared.

| DIE NUMBERS | | | | | | | |
|---|---|---|---|---|---|---|---|
| CASINO | 1 | 2 | 3 | 4 | 5 | 6 | TOTAL DIE ROLLS |
| Frontier | 326 | 402 | 366 | 345 | 351 | 368 | 2,158 |
| Hilton | 312 | 316 | 296 | 323 | 294 | 319 | 1,860 |
| Caesars | 498 | 524 | 559 | 540 | 493 | 482 | 3,096 |
| Sands | 485 | 519 | 494 | 491 | 470 | 463 | 2,922 |
| Nugget | 877 | 886 | 891 | 891 | 854 | 873 | 5,272 |
| 40-Hour Totals | 2,498 | 2,647 | 2,606 | 2,590 | 2,462 | 2,505 | 15,308 |
| Probability | 2,551 | 2,551 | 2,551 | 2,551 | 2,551 | 2,551 | |

In presenting this data, the theoretical dice probabilities for each casino were not shown, only the theoretical probabilities for the total 40 hours. This same procedure will be followed for all the tabulations in this book. The theoretical probabilities for each casino can be calculated easily should you wish to do so. However, in craps, your overall performance will be determined by how well you perform as a total at all the crap tables in all the casinos in which you gamble, not just in one or two among them. This is the way that most players shoot craps—a little time at one table, followed by short times at other tables.

When the two dice are rolled, one die will come to rest with one of its six sides on top and the other die will come to rest also with one of its six sides on top. The sum of these two numbers will be some number from 2 to 12. If a one appears on the top of each die, the dice number is 2.

There is only one combination of the dice that can produce a 2. Likewise, there is only one way that two 2's can produce a 4, that two 3's can produce a 6, and two 4's can make an 8, that two 5's can make a 10, and two 6's a 12.

There are two ways that each other combination of two numbers can be constructed. For example, a 3 can consist of a 1 on the first die and a 2 on the second die, or it can consist of a 2 on the first die and a 1 on the second die. We can now construct a chart that shows all these various combinations of numbers that a pair of dice can produce.

## COMBINATIONS OF THE DICE

| NUMBER THROWN | COMBINATIONS | NUMBER OF COMBINATIONS |
|---|---|---|
| 2 | | 1 |
| 3 | | 2 |
| 4 | | 3 |
| 5 | | 4 |
| 6 | | 5 |
| 7 | | 6 |
| 8 | | 5 |
| 9 | | 4 |
| 10 | | 3 |
| 11 | | 2 |
| 12 | | 1 |

From the foregoing chart we can see that there are 21 number combinations produced by the two dice and there are 36 dice combinations produced by the two dice.

# DICE COMBINATIONS

Let's now tabulate the quantities of dice combinations produced by the dice with all their rolls at the five casinos and compare these with their theoretical probabilities.

| DICE COMBINATIONS | | Frontier | Hilton | Caesars | Sands | Nugget | 40/hr/total | Probability |
|---|---|---|---|---|---|---|---|---|
| 2 | (1-1) | 31 | 34 | 43 | 35 | 67 | 210 | 213 |
| 3 | (1-2) | 60 | 53 | 85 | 78 | 157 | 433 | 425 |
| 4 | (2-2) | 36 | 33 | 48 | 39 | 69 | 225 | 213 |
| | (1-3) | 45 | 46 | 99 | 82 | 159 | 431 | 425 |
| 5 | (1-4) | 47 | 58 | 70 | 87 | 141 | 403 | 425 |
| | (2-3) | 71 | 51 | 85 | 99 | 149 | 455 | 425 |
| 6 | (3-3) | 31 | 25 | 35 | 38 | 73 | 202 | 213 |
| | (1-5) | 53 | 57 | 69 | 78 | 142 | 399 | 425 |
| | (2-4) | 75 | 49 | 97 | 91 | 152 | 464 | 425 |
| 7 | (1-6) | 59 | 30 | 89 | 90 | 144 | 412 | 425 |
| | (2-5) | 55 | 45 | 85 | 90 | 146 | 421 | 425 |
| | (3-4) | 52 | 52 | 110 | 77 | 141 | 432 | 425 |
| 8 | (4-4) | 24 | 23 | 49 | 48 | 70 | 214 | 213 |
| | (2-6) | 69 | 52 | 76 | 83 | 144 | 424 | 425 |
| | (3-5) | 75 | 49 | 94 | 74 | 137 | 429 | 425 |
| 9 | (3-6) | 61 | 48 | 101 | 86 | 159 | 455 | 425 |
| | (4-5) | 56 | 51 | 81 | 69 | 155 | 412 | 425 |
| 10 | (5-5) | 33 | 15 | 44 | 44 | 65 | 201 | 213 |
| | (4-6) | 67 | 67 | 84 | 71 | 162 | 457 | 425 |
| 11 | (5-6) | 46 | 62 | 76 | 71 | 144 | 399 | 425 |
| 12 | (6-6) | 33 | 30 | 28 | 31 | 60 | 182 | 213 |

In the basic game of craps, we are not concerned with the composition of the numbers. We are concerned only with the sum of the numbers on the two dice. Consequently, we can take the foregoing outline of the various dice combinations, which total 36, and consolidate them further.

# DICE PROBABILITIES AND EXPECTATIONS

Take a look at the following probability chart.

| PROBABILITY | |
|---|---|
| One way to make a 2 | 1/36 |
| Two ways to make a 3 | 2/36 |
| Three ways to make a 4 | 3/36 |
| Four ways to make a 5 | 4/36 |
| Five ways to make a 6 | 5/36 |
| Six ways to make a 7 | 6/36 |
| Five ways to make an 8 | 5/36 |
| Four ways to make a 9 | 4/36 |
| Three ways to make a 10 | 3/36 |
| Two ways to make an 11 | 2/36 |
| One way to make a 12 | 1/36 |

This chart shows us that each complementary pair of numbers has the same probability: 2 and 12 (1/36), 3 and 11 (2/36), 4 and 10 (3/36), 5 and 9 (4/36), 6 and 8 (5/36), and 7 and 7 (6/36).

Now take a look at the next chart, which shows how the dice performances at all five casinos adhered to their probabilities.

| SUM OF BOTH DICE | | | | | | | | | | | | |
|---|---|---|---|---|---|---|---|---|---|---|---|---|
| | 2 | 3 | 4 | 5 | 6 | 7 | 8 | 9 | 10 | 11 | 12 | TOTALS |
| **Frontier** | 31 | 60 | 81 | 118 | 159 | 166 | 168 | 117 | 100 | 46 | 33 | 1,079 |
| **Hilton** | 34 | 53 | 79 | 109 | 131 | 127 | 124 | 99 | 82 | 62 | 30 | 930 |
| **Caesars** | 43 | 85 | 147 | 155 | 201 | 284 | 219 | 182 | 128 | 76 | 28 | 1,548 |
| **Sands** | 35 | 78 | 121 | 186 | 207 | 257 | 205 | 155 | 115 | 71 | 31 | 1,461 |
| **Nugget** | 67 | 157 | 228 | 290 | 367 | 431 | 351 | 314 | 227 | 144 | 60 | 2,636 |
| **40/hr/ total** | 210 | 433 | 656 | 858 | 1065 | 1265 | 1067 | 867 | 652 | 399 | 182 | 7,654 |
| **Prob- ability** | 213 | 425 | 638 | 850 | 1063 | 1276 | 1063 | 850 | 638 | 425 | 213 | |

# CONCLUSIONS

In this chapter we have shown that in producing numbers, dice perform close to what theory dictates they should. No consistent performance of the number on any one die, nor did the performance of any of the numbers produced by both dice, show any consistent non-probability performance at any casino to a degree that could have led to the development of any winning gambling scheme. The dice performed as they should. It is essential that we accept this fact when attempting to establish a winning course of betting.

# 5 THE BASIC GAME AND ITS ODDS

Most people learn about the game of craps by playing the game first with friends at home, acquaintances in a back alley, players in a casino, buddies in the armed forces, or wherever someone pulls out a pair of dice and suggests a game. The game itself is always the same, one in which people squat or kneel in a circle on the floor, or stand around a casino table.

## HOME GAMES AND CASINO GAMES

In home games and other types of non-casino crap games, the shooter determines the size of the betting pool by offering an amount that the other participants can match with bets. Matching someone else's bet is called "fading." Any amount that is not matched is returned to the shooter before he makes his first roll of the dice. Sometimes, side bets are made between participants, and sometimes odds are offered with these side bets. However, no bets can be made unless there are people in the game willing to cover or **fade** them.

In private games, players bet against the shooter's ability to make a **pass**, craps terminology for "win." The betting is against the shooter, who is the person that rolls the dice.

In casino games, the basic game is the same except that all bets are made against the house. A person may place bets against the shooter's ability to make a pass, or with his ability to make a pass. Most betting is with the shooter's ability to make a pass. When a player makes a bet against the shooter's ability to make a pass, he makes what is called a **don't pass bet**.

## THE BASIC GAME

The basic game, whether it is a "fading" game or a casino game, has a shooter making the first roll of the dice, referred to as **coming out**. With this first roll, if the shooter throws a **natural** (a 7 or an 11), he wins his bet, and he may then make a new bet and begin a new point with a new coming out roll.

On the other hand, if he rolls a **crap** on his first roll (a 2, 3, or 12), he loses his bet, but does not "lose the dice" (give them up to another player), and he is free to make another bet and try again. On the first roll, if he throws neither a natural nor a crap, he establishes a **point** (a 4, 5, 6, 8, 9, or 10).

Following his establishing a point, the shooter continues to roll the dice until he either rolls his point or a 7. If he rolls his point before rolling a 7, he wins his bet, "keeps the dice" (continues to roll), makes a new bet, and comes out with a new first roll. However, after establishing his point, if he rolls a 7 before rolling his point, he loses his bet and he loses the dice, passing them to the person to his left, who then makes a bet and comes out with a first roll of the dice.

After establishing a point on the first roll, should the roller throw an 11 or a crap on any of the following rolls, the 11 or the crap would have no effect on either his winning or losing his bet. After a point has been established, winning or losing his bet depends entirely upon the rolling of the point or the rolling of a 7, whichever comes first.

The game of craps is a game of decisions. A player must make decisions about how much he wishes to bet, and in the casino game which has a large variety of betting opportunities, he must make decisions as to which betting opportunities he wishes to play. In addition to his decisions about how he will bet, the player who is shooting the dice must also make a decision as to how he will throw the dice—throw them high, throw them hard, or any other way he chooses.

But when the dice leave the shooter's hand, the decision making of the shooter and of all the other players ceases. The dice now take over and make the decisions that will lead to whether the players win or lose.

Craps is not a competition between the skills of people, one pitted against the other. It is a competition between a person's skill or luck at betting against or with the decision making of the dice which, in turn, is determined by the mathematical probabilities that the markings on the dice present.

## THE COMING OUT ROLL

On the coming out roll the dice may present us with a natural or a crap, in which case the dice will have decided in one roll whether we win or lose, depending upon how we had bet. With the coming out roll, the dice may establish a point, in which case it will take more rolls of the dice before a winning decision or a losing decision is made by the dice.

> Craps is a competition between your skill or luck at betting against or with the decision making of the dice which, in turn, is determined by the mathematical probabilities of the dice.

Regardless whether it takes one roll or a large number of rolls before a win or lose decision is reached, we will consider that all of the rolls that take place in reaching a single win or lose conclusion are merely parts of a single decision. In describing different decisions we will title these according to the type of bet upon which the dice will be called upon to render a decision.

For example, a **pass bet decision** refers to a bet that has been placed to pass on the casino table and gets completed as either a winning or losing bet. A **don't pass bet decision** refers to a bet that has been placed to don't pass and gets completed as either a winning or losing bet. There are also many others, such as field bet decisions, come bet decisions, hardway bet decisions, and so on. In the private game there is basically one decision—the pass bet decision—because that is the only choice the shooter has been given.

A **hand** contains all the rolls of the dice that a shooter throws, including the 7 that causes him to lose his last point and pass the dice. In a hand there may be many different win and loss decisions such as hardway bet decisions, come bet decisions, and so on, but pass bet decisions are the only decisions that are considered in the win and loss divisions of the hand.

A hand cannot be concluded on a coming out roll. Neither a 7 or 11 on the coming-out roll, which wins a pass bet decision, or a 2, 3, or 12 (a craps), which loses, ends the hand. It merely concludes a pass bet decision and starts another pass bet decision and coming-out roll. A *hand* ends only when a 7 is thrown on any roll other than a coming-out roll, a loss on the pass—in other words, a point has been established and now loses ending the hand. As you see, a hand cannot be concluded on just one throw and it can consist of more than one pass bet decision.

The procedure of making bets, coming out, winning bets and keeping the dice, losing bets and losing the dice, and passing the dice is the same whether you're betting in a fading game or betting at the casino table. The odds against the shooter **making a pass** (throwing a natural on the first roll or making his point) are the same in either game—1,004 to 976 against winning.

## THE ODDS ON PASS BETS

Odds against winning are often stated as 251 to 244, which is merely a reduction of the 1,004 to 976 ratio to its smallest fraction. For the purposes of this book the odds against winning with pass bets will always be stated as 1,004 to 976.

It might seem from the odds of 1,004 to 976 against the shooter that to bet against the shooter would be a certain way of winning, but this is not necessarily true. In the fading game, for example, the first person to have the opportunity of covering the shooter's bet is the last person to have rolled the dice. That person is the first person to the shooter's right, and if he does not cover all of the bet, the options for fading what money remains progresses to the right until all of it has been covered.

If any of the shooter's bet is not covered by the players, the amount that has not been faded is handed back to him. If all of the bet is faded before all the players have had a turn to fade, these remaining players have no way of betting against the shooter. Consequently, a player in the private game is not privileged to bet against the dice on every roll or to bet any amount against the dice that he may wish. The odds of 1,004 to 976 are predicated on the assumption a unit bet is made each time the dice come out and that this unit bet is faded by a unit bet of the same size.

It may appear that betting against the dice in the private game should give a certain winning result because the odds favor losing. Technically this is true, but for reasons that will become obvious later, the formula for winning big in the fading game is to bet as little as possible against the roller. Instead, the player should rely entirely upon his own rolling of the dice.

# HOT HANDS

Many "hot hands" will appear every evening. The chances for one player to have a "hot" roll are the same as for any other player. The action that decides who becomes the big winner in the fading game during one evening depends upon who makes the most of his big and little "hot hands."

There is not time enough in one evening for the losing decisions to add to a sizeable win. For example, if 1,980 pass bet decisions were to be concluded and should these result in a distribution of wins and losses in proportion to the odds, there would be 1,004 losses and 976 wins, which is 28 more losses than wins. If the betting unit against the shooters had been $1, a person betting against the dice would have won $28. A $5 unit would have produced $140 winnings.

1,980 pass bet decisions would take more than 24 hours to complete. Reducing the game to six hours give returns of $7 and $35. Next, if we assume that the don't pass bettor was only able to place bets on one-half of these decisions, his possible winnings for the six hours would be $3.50 and $17.50. Need we say more about betting against the shooter in the private game?

In order to win big in the private game when betting against the dice, a person must bet big, and since the player who fades the shooter has no say in how large the amount might be that he can fade against, he has no certainty that he will always have, or even ever have, a large amount of bet money offered.

# A MAJOR DIFFERENCE

The major difference between the fading game and the game offered in the casino is that a player in the casino game can make bets on every coming out roll in the game in any amount that he desires, between the minimum and the maximum limits set by the casino, and he can bet either with the shooter making passes or against his making passes (don't pass).

The odds of 1,004 to 976 against making a pass apply to both games. But in the casino game the odds against winning when betting against the shooter making his pass (don't pass bet) are 976 to 949, rather than 976 to 1,004 as they are in the fading game. This might seem confusing.

If the casino changed nothing to alter the natural odds, the odds for winning by betting don't pass would be 1,004 to 976 in favor of the bettor. This would be bad for the house, so the casino will specify that when a 12 (or it could be a 2) is rolled on the coming out roll, the bets made to pass still lose, the same as before, thus leaving the odds at 1,004 to 976 against winning on pass, but the bets made on don't pass neither win nor lose.

Since probability says that a 12 will appear once for each 36 rolls, and since there will be 1,980 (1,004 losses + 976 wins) coming out rolls of the dice, the number of probable 12's will be 55 (calculated by dividing 1,980 by 36). This makes 949 (calculated by subtracting 55 from 1,004) winning rolls for don't pass bets. Thus, the odds are 976 to 949 against winning on a don't pass bet at the casino table.

Before proceeding further, we should examine the meaning of three very important words that we will encounter during the remainder of this book—*probability*, *odds*, and *return*. The next chapter explains these three basic mathematical concepts in detail.

# 6 THREE IMPORTANT CONCEPTS IN CRAPS

Throughout this book, we will be discussing three mathematical concepts that are vital to your understanding of the game of craps. They may sound imposing, but I assure you that they can be easily explained and understood. These three concepts—probability, odds, and return—are the reasons why some bets that you can make at the crap table are far better than other bets. Basically, it's a money matter—you can make more money or lose less money on your bets, depending on their probability, odds and return.

## PROBABILITY

The mathematical probability for having something occur is the ratio of the number of times that this event is likely to happen compared to the whole number of ways of which this particular event is a part.

For example, we can say that the probability for having two dice add to two is 1 out of 36 rolls, because out of the 36 possible combinations of the two dice, only one of them adds to two.

# ODDS

The mathematical odds for having something occur is the ratio of the number of times an event is likely to happen compared to the number of times the event is likely not to happen out of the whole number of ways of which these particular events are parts.

For example, out of the 36 possible combinations on a pair of dice, only one of them can add to 2. This leaves 35 dice combinations that do not add to 2. Consequently, the odds against a single roll of the dice resulting in a 2 are 35 to 1, not 36 to 1 as some people falsely state.

# RETURN

The return is simply the total amount returned to the bettor after he wins a bet. The return is the sum of the amount he bet plus the amount he won. For example, if you bet $1 that a 2 will be rolled on the next roll of the dice and if you're given the correct odds of 35 to 1, if you roll a 2 you would be paid winnings of $35. Added to your bet of $1, you would have a return of $36.

The crap tables do not pay 35 to 1 odds for a bet on the number 2. Instead, most of them state a payoff of "30 for 1," which means that for each dollar bet on a winning 2, there will be a return of $30. Since one of those dollars will be the one that was bet, the odds that the casino is giving are actually 29 to 1, not the 30 to 1 that they would like us to believe.

# RETURN RATIO

The return ratio for a bet is the ratio of what the total return actually is compared to what it would have been had its true odds been applied to its winning amount. For example, when $30 is returned for a winning bet on 2 when $36 would be the return at the true odds, the return ratio paid by the casino is 83.333% (30 ÷ 36 x 100).

Now let's compute the return ratios for the basic game of craps, based on the odds of 1,004 to 976 against pass:

When 976 wins are realized, and since 976 were bet in order to realize these wins, the return is 976 + 976 = 1,952. The total number of bets is 1,004 + 976 = 1,980. Therefore, the pass return ratio is 1952/1980 x 100 = 98.59%, often stated as 98.6%, and quite often mistakenly called the "odds for craps" instead of the return ratio. The don't come return ratio is (949 + 949) ÷ (976 + 949) x 100 = 98.59%.

What these return ratios of 98.59% mean is that for every $100 bet to pass or to don't pass in craps, the probability is that $98.59 will be returned, making a probability loss of $1.41 for each $100 bet.

Returns and return ratios are what we are interested in when shooting craps, and so we will use return and return ratio, and not odds, when comparing different bets and methods of betting.

When we observe a return of $98.59 for each $100 bet, it is puzzling how some bettors are able to lose so much money so quickly at the casino crap tables. Later we will discuss the many bets other than pass and don't pass that you can make on a casino table. We will develop their return ratios, and discuss the ways that most losing bettors misplay them.

> Bettors lose heavily because they do not understand the relationship between the probabilities for bets and their returns.

Now let's compare the actual results from the five casinos with their probabilities. There were a total of 2,219 coming out rolls of the dice. These should have distributed themselves into numbers in proportion to what the probabilities of the 36 combinations of the dice dictate. Take a look at this chart.

| POINT NUMBERS FOR COMING OUT ROLLS | | | | | | | | | | | |
|---|---|---|---|---|---|---|---|---|---|---|---|
| | **2** | **3** | **4** | **5** | **6** | **7** | **8** | **9** | **10** | **11** | **12** |
| **Frontier** | 10 | 18 | 22 | 38 | 49 | 40 | 50 | 30 | 22 | 14 | 6 |
| **Hilton** | 4 | 13 | 21 | 42 | 42 | 25 | 20 | 26 | 26 | 11 | 5 |
| **Caesars** | 15 | 35 | 49 | 41 | 63 | 96 | 62 | 60 | 38 | 29 | 9 |
| **Sands** | 13 | 27 | 47 | 52 | 67 | 76 | 58 | 48 | 38 | 17 | 7 |
| **Nugget** | 18 | 43 | 73 | 82 | 108 | 120 | 96 | 77 | 64 | 44 | 15 |
| **Total** | **60** | **136** | **212** | **255** | **329** | **357** | **286** | **241** | **187** | **115** | **42** |
| **Probability** | **61½** | **123** | **185** | **247** | **308** | **370** | **308** | **247** | **185** | **123** | **61½** |

Some of these coming out rolls resulted in passes (wins). Some produced losses. The following chart is a tabulation of how this distribution of wins and losses at the five casinos compared to their probabilities.

| WINS & LOSSES COMPARED TO PROBABILITIES | | | | | | | |
|---|---|---|---|---|---|---|---|
| | **FRONTIER** | **HILTON** | **CAESARS** | **SANDS** | **NUGGET** | **TOTAL** | **PROB** |
| **Winning 7's** | 40 | 25 | 96 | 76 | 120 | 357 | 370 |
| **Winning 11's** | 14 | 11 | 29 | 17 | 44 | 115 | 123 |
| **Winning 4's** | 7 | 8 | 17 | 15 | 21 | 68 | 61½ |
| **Winning 5's** | 14 | 21 | 13 | 25 | 34 | 107 | 99½ |
| **Winning 6's** | 21 | 19 | 25 | 40 | 37 | 142 | 140 |
| **Winning 8's** | 26 | 8 | 29 | 18 | 40 | 121 | 140 |
| **Winning 9's** | 12 | 10 | 23 | 19 | 32 | 96 | 99½ |
| **Winning 10's** | 5 | 8 | 18 | 12 | 25 | 68 | 61½ |
| **Losing 2's** | 10 | 4 | 15 | 13 | 18 | 60 | 61½ |
| **Losing 3's** | 18 | 13 | 35 | 27 | 43 | 136 | 123 |
| **Losing 12's** | 6 | 5 | 9 | 7 | 15 | 42 | 61½ |
| **Losing 4's** | 15 | 13 | 32 | 32 | 52 | 144 | 123 |
| **Losing 5's** | 24 | 21 | 28 | 27 | 48 | 148 | 148 |
| **Losing 6's** | 28 | 23 | 38 | 27 | 71 | 187 | 168 |
| **Losing 8's** | 24 | 12 | 33 | 40 | 56 | 165 | 168 |
| **Losing 9's** | 18 | 16 | 37 | 29 | 45 | 145 | 148 |
| **Losing 10's** | 17 | 17 | 20 | 26 | 39 | 119 | 123 |

# WHAT THE TABULATIONS SHOW

These tabulations show that during the 40 hours at the five casinos, the dice kept very close relationships with their pass bet decisions and with what their probabilities indicated they should. This gives further evidence that the dice will perform in accordance to what mathematical probability dictates. They will not warp their performances to agree with what some crap addict's fantasies hope they will.

For the five casinos, there were 1,074 pass wins and 1,146 pass losses. When we subtract the 42 coming out 12's from the 1,146 pass losses, we get 1,104 don't pass wins. These compute to:

**96.76% Return Ratio for Pass**

$$(1074 + 1074) \div (1146 + 1074) \times 100 = 96.76\%$$

**101.38% Return Ratio for Don't Pass**

$$(1104+1104) \div (1074 + 1104) \times 100 = 101.38\%$$

These return ratios compare favorably with the 98.59% theoretical return ratios for both pass and don't pass.

# WHAT THE RETURN RATIO PERCENTS SHOW

- 96.76% says that for each $100 bet, the loss should be $3.24.
- For the 2,220 total decisions at the five casinos, the loss should have been 3.24 x 2,220/100 = $72.
- Of the 2,220 coming out rolls, 1,074 wins and 1,146 losses were produced. $1,146–$1,074 = $72 loss.

- 101.38 % says that for each $100 bet, the profit should be $1.38.
- For the 2,178 total opportunities (2,220–42 twelves), the don't pass profit should have been $1.38 x 2178/100 = $30.
- Of the 2,220 coming out rolls, 1104 don't pass wins and 1074 don't pass losses were produced. $1104–$1074 = $30 win.

Because these return ratios give calculated returns that agree with the actual returns, we use return ratio as our measure for comparing the results that the various bets offered by the casino crap tables give.

The 40 hours of crap table data recorded at the five casinos shows the following statement to be true.

> Dice perform very closely to what probability says that they should. This is essential to an understanding of how to beat the game.

Had one more hour been spent at each casino, perhaps the final results would have shown a higher return for pass than for don't pass. This is mere speculation, though my statistical analysis has shown that the dice are always reacting quickly toward reversing all unbalances so as to bring them back to balance.

The 2,200 pass bet decisions completed with the dice in the five casinos spanned 40 hours. However, in a private game these probably would have taken about 30 hours since no time would have been wasted in the private game for handling come bets, place bets, or the other casino bets. During these 2,220 decisions, the dice produced many more losers than what theoretical probability would dictate. The pass return ratio was 96.76%, compared to the theoretical probability of 98.59%.

It gave a loss ratio of 3.24% compared to the theoretical probability loss of 1.41 %, which makes it 2.3 times as great as the theoretical.

The total loss would have been $72 for $1 bets over a 30-hour period in the private game which, when reduced to six hours, would have been $15. This figure would have been further reduced to $7.50 if a 50% participation rate had been considered for a private game, ($37.50 if the betting had been $5).

Actual results, even when they favor betting against the dice by as much as 2.3 times the probability, do not show that betting against the shooter in the private game is the way to become a big winner.

In the next chapter, we will take a look at some more types of casino crap wagers called "contract bets," and discuss how they differ from other bets.

# 7 PASS AND COME: THE CONTRACT BETS

On the casino crap table, you can pick up your don't pass and don't come bets and remove them from the game at any time. Therefore, don't pass and don't come bets are not "contract" bets. However, pass and come bets are **contract bets**—they cannot be removed until a conclusion to the point has been reached.

If you could remove your pass and come bets from the casino table after they had been established as points, you could adjust the odds to favor your winning. For example, when the dice are coming out, you could place one bet on pass and a similar bet on don't pass. If a 7, 11, 2 or 3 were thrown on the first roll, you would win one bet and lose the other, thus breaking even. If a 12 were thrown on the coming out roll, you would lose the pass bet while having no action on your don't pass bet, in which case you would lose 55 times out of 1,980 coming out rolls.

## THE PASS BET

When we consider the basic probabilities of the casino game, we see that 660 rolls would be retired on the coming out roll, 440 by naturals and 220 by craps. This means that 1,320 points would be established whose fates would be determined by future rolls. Out of these 1,320 points, 536 of them would become pass wins, and 784 would become don't pass wins.

If a bettor places bets both to pass and to don't pass on the 1,980 coming out rolls, he would have a net loss of 55 on these coming out rolls. If he next would remove all his pass bets that remained after the coming out roll, he would have 1,320 don't pass bets when the second roll began. Of these 1,320 don't pass bets, he would lose 536 of them due to passes, and he would win 784 of them. His total loss would be $536 + $55 coming-out 12's = $591, which, when subtracted from his $784 don't pass wins, would leave a $193 profit.

This method of betting would create a return ratio of:

$$(784 + 784) \div (591 + 784) \times 100 = 114\%$$

When we look at this potential return ratio of 114%, we can easily understand why the casino pass and come bets are contract bets that cannot be removed.

Had the pass bets been left and the don't pass bets removed after the coming out rolls, the result would have been a return ratio of:

$$(536 + 536) \div (784 + 55) + 536 \times 100 = 77.96\%$$

When we look at this 77.96% return ratio, we can understand why the casino permits the don't pass and don't come bets to be removed.

The casino is in business to make money. Its income depends upon the amount of money its customers bet, less the return given to them. Consequently, the lower the return that a bet will probably yield, the more profitable it should be for the casino.

> The casino will never refuse a customer the opportunity to lower his probable return ratio percent!

The casino will never refuse a customer the opportunity to lower his probable return ratio percent! Every time you pick up an already established don't pass or a don't come bet, you improve the possible yield to the casinos by a very, very, very large percent!

# THE COME BET

Bets that begin with a roll other than the first one are known as come bets. On any roll of the dice after the coming out roll, you can begin a come bet decision by placing a bet in the large box marked "Come" on the table.

The rules for the come bet are the same as the rules for the pass bet. If a 7 or 11 is rolled on the first roll after the come bet has been placed (a **come bet coming out roll**), the bettor wins. If a crap is rolled, he loses. If neither of these happens, a **come point** is established that will win if the come point number is rolled before a 7 is rolled, and it will lose if a 7 is rolled first.

You can also make don't come bets, placing them at any time after the first roll.

# PASS AND COME ANALYSIS

The pass and come bets are contract bets. They must be left on the table until the point has been concluded with either a win or a loss. The don't pass and don't come bets are not contract bets. They can be removed at any time.

Now comes a test to determine how knowledgeable you have become about the probabilities of the game of craps. Can you say what the probable result should be if a gambler were to place a bet on every roll of the dice—a pass bet with every first roll of the dice and a come bet with each other roll? Are the odds of 1,004 to 976 against making pass the same for the come bets?

Before stating a conclusion let's see what the result would have been had a bettor placed these bets on every one of the

7,654 rolls of the dice at the five casinos. We will tabulate the results for both the pass and come bet cases and for the don't pass and don't come cases.

| RESULTS FOR PASS & DON'T PASS | | | | |
|---|---|---|---|---|
| | PASS | | DON'T PASS | |
| | WIN | LOSE | WIN | LOSE |
| Frontier | 139 | 160 | 154 | 139 |
| Hilton | 110 | 124 | 119 | 110 |
| Caesars | 250 | 247 | 238 | 250 |
| Sands | 222 | 228 | 221 | 222 |
| Nugget | 353 | 387 | 372 | 353 |
| 40-Hour Total | 1074 | 1146 | 1104 | 1074 |
| Return Ratio | 96.76% | | 101.38% | |
| | $(1074 + 1074) \div (1074 + 1146) \times 100 = 96.76\%$ | | $(1104 + 1104) \div (1104+1074) \times 100 = 101.38\%$ | |

| RESULTS FOR COME & DON'T COME | | | | |
|---|---|---|---|---|
| | COME | | DON'T COME | |
| | WIN | LOSE | WIN | LOSE |
| Frontier | 382 | 398 | 371 | 382 |
| Hilton | 355 | 341 | 316 | 355 |
| Caesars | 534 | 518 | 499 | 534 |
| Sands | 506 | 505 | 481 | 506 |
| Nugget | 953 | 943 | 898 | 953 |
| 40-Hour Total | 2730 | 2705 | 2565 | 2730 |
| Return Ratio | 100.46% | | 96.88% | |
| | $(2730 + 2730) \div (2730 + 2705) \times 100 = 100.46\%$ | | $(2565 + 2565) \div (2565 + 2730) \times 100 = 96.88\%$ | |

# PASS & COME: THE CONTRACT BETS

If a bettor had placed bets on all the possible pass and come bets or on all of the possible don't pass and don't come bets, the results would have been:

| RESULTS FOR PASS & DON'T PASS | | | | |
|---|---|---|---|---|
| | PASS + COME | | DON'T PASS + DON'T COME | |
| | WIN | LOSE | WIN | LOSE |
| 40-Hour Total | 3804 | 3851 | 3609 | 3804 |
| Return Ratio | 99.39% | | 98.19% | |
| | (3804 + 3804) ÷ (3804 + 3851) x 100 = 99.39% | | (3669 + 3669) ÷ (3669 + 3804) x 100 = 98.19% | |

The odds against winning with come bets is the same as that against winning with pass bets—1,004 to 976—and the return ratio for come and don't come bets has the same probability as for pass and don't pass, 98.59%. Once again the dice have shown that, given a few rolls, they will maintain their basic probabilities.

Another point to be emphasized is that each category of bets is independent in its results from any other bet category. Pass bets and come bets both have the same basic structures, except that pass bets always commence with the first roll whereas come bets can be started at any roll other than the first.

The results for the 40 hours at the five casinos showed a pass return ratio less than the probability of 98.59% and a come bet return ratio greater than the probability of 98.59%. There was no reason why the come bet return ratio could not also have been less

> Pass bets and come bets both have the same basic structures, except that pass bets always commence with the first roll whereas come bets can be started at any roll other than the first.

than the probability return ratio of 98.59%. Each acts independently of the other.

Crap players who relish the rush they get from gambling on exotic wagers with long odds against them make other types of bets generally known as **sucker bets**. We will investigate the sucker bets in craps, as well as the trap bets, and discuss their odds in the next chapter.

# 8 TRAP AND SUCKER BETS

The casino crap table offers many bets in addition to the basic ones of pass, don't pass, come and don't come. These other glittering little bargains are what produce the large profits for the house. Without them the casino would have difficulty paying for the operation of the crap table. The casino's 1.41% take from the total money bet on the basic game would be very meager unless there were many high bettors at the table.

Let's examine 15 additional casino crap table bets, and discuss their efficacy.

## A. TRAP BETS

### COME AND DON'T COME

We know that the return ratio for come bets is the same as that for pass, 98.59%. This means that the probable loss for a bettor who plays the come bets will be $1.41 for each $100 he bets, the same as it is for pass. But, if you place come bets at every opportunity, your loss will be much greater than if you were to limit yourself to pass bets only.

The average number of dice rolls in a pass bet decision computes to 3.36. As a consequence, it will take 6,653 (1980 x 3.36) dice rolls to complete 1,980 pass bet decisions. We have shown that the 1,980 pass bet decisions would be made up of

1,004 losses and 976 wins, so that if you bet pass for 1,980 coming out rolls, you would create a loss of 28 betting units (1004 – 976). We could also compute this by multiplying the number of bets by the loss percent of 1.41% (100% - 98.59%), which would also give us a loss of 28 betting units (1,980 x 1.41% = 28).

If you were to bet come only and never bet pass, you would have the opportunity (since you could not place a come bet on a pass coming out roll) of placing 4,673 come bets (6,653–1,980). This would produce a probable come bet loss of 66 betting units (4,673 x 1.41%).

If you were to place both pass and come bets on every opportunity that 6,653 rolls of the dice would give you, you would face a probability loss of 94 betting units (28 pass + 66 come = 94 or 6,653 x 1.41% = 94).

A bettor who is betting don't come would have only 4,543 opportunities for betting don't come because of the 130 12's that would appear during the 4,673 rolls of the dice. This would give him only 64 don't come probability unit betting losses. Adding these 64 to his don't pass probability loss of 27 (976 – 949) would give him a total of 91 (27 + 64) for his don't pass and don't come bets.

*Trap bets give you the chance to increase the rate at which you can lose money.*

From the foregoing, we can see the principle behind all the additional bets—the trap bets—that casinos offer. Even though the return ratios for some of them are the same as for pass and don't pass, these trap bets offer the player opportunities for increasing the rate at which he can lose his money!

## ODDS BET WITH PASS AND COME

After a point (4, 5, 6, 8, 9, 10) has been established on the first pass or come roll, you can place a bet of equal size to back up your bet. On a pass bet, you will place your bet behind the pass line, directly behind your bet. On a come bet, you will give your bet to the dealer, who will place it slightly off center on top of your come bet, so that it can be recognized easily as being an odds bet if the point is made and a payoff is due.

These additional bets are odds bets, and the casino pays the correct odds on them. For example, there are three ways to roll a 4 and six ways to roll a 7. Therefore, the correct odds are 2 to 1 against the shooter rolling a 4 before he rolls a 7. Consequently, assuming a $1 bet, if a 4 is established as the point on the coming out roll and if an odds bet of $1 is placed behind the line followed by a 4 being rolled to make a winning point, the payoff would be as follows: a $1 win for the original $1 pass bet plus a $2 win for the odds bet, making a total of $3 won for $2 bet—or a return of $5 for $2 bet.

The odds for 10 are the same as for 4; that is, 2 to 1 against making the point. The odds with 5 and 9 are 3 to 2 (four ways to roll a 5 or a 9, and six ways to roll a 7). The odds on 6 and 8 are 6 to 5 (five ways to roll a 6 or an 8 and six ways to roll a 7).

| ODDS AGAINST MAKING THE POINT | | |
| --- | --- | --- |
| NUMBER | WAYS TO ROLL | ODDS |
| 4 | 3 | 2 to 1 |
| 5 | 4 | 3 to 2 |
| 6 | 5 | 6 to 5 |
| 8 | 5 | 6 to 5 |
| 9 | 4 | 3 to 2 |
| 10 | 3 | 2 to 1 |
| Note: There are six ways to roll a 7, which is a loser for odds bets on the pass and come. | | |

If we examine these odds, we see that a $1 bet can be backed with a $1 odds bet if the point is 4 or 10. However, if the point is 5 or 9, the original bet would have to be at least $2 if it is to be backed with an odds bet unless the casino makes payments in half dollars. If the point is 6 or 8, the original bet must be at least $5 in order that the 6 to 5 odds can be paid in even dollars.

This means that if you wish to back all your pass and come bets, you will have to limit your minimum bet to $5 with most of your bigger bets in $5 multiples. Why? Because when you place your pass or come bet, you don't know which point number might be rolled, so you must protect yourself against the possibility of having a 6 or an 8 becoming the point.

Backing bets with odds bets is one of the first new bets that a crap player learns on his road to sophistication. By the nature of the odds structure, he is coerced in increasing his betting unit up from the $1 or $2 table minimum to the glittering $5 chips.

## DOUBLE ODDS

Some casinos permit **double odds**. This means that you can place an odds bet that is twice as large as your pass or come bet. The payouts for these are at the same correct odds as for the single odds bets. For example, if a $1 bet had a 4 for a point and a double odds bet of $2 were placed behind the line, the return for the $3 would be $8 ($1 win on pass, plus $1 bet on pass, plus $4 win on the $2 odds bet, plus the $2 that had been bet on the odds).

Backing our pass bets with single odds bets will increase our return ratio from 98.59% to 99.15%. This means that we have decreased our loss percentage from 1.41% down to 0.85%. Hoorah for us! We have decreased our loss percent from each roll of the dice, but in doing this we have not decreased our actual loss. We have been forced to increase our betting amount from 1,980 units to 3,300 (1,980 + 1,320) units. This means that our loss, which was 28 units (1,980 x 1.41 % = 28) has remained at 28 units (3,300 x 0.85% = 28).

To put it another way, we have risked more money and we are no better off than if we had not added odds bets to our betting repertoire!

Now let's look at what the results would have been if single odds bets had been placed behind each pass point in the five casinos:

| SINGLE ODDS RESULTS FOR PASS | | |
|---|---|---|
| | RETURN | BET |
| Frontier | 482.40 | 510 |
| Hilton | 404.90 | 410 |
| Caesars | 811.80 | 809 |
| Sands | 758.40 | 760 |
| Nugget | 1,173.90 | 1,239 |
| 40-Hour Total | 3,631.40 | 3,728. |
| Return Ratio | 97.41% | |

Here is the math:

Return (3,631.40) ÷ Amount Bet (3,728.00) x 100 = 97.41%.

This appears to be an improvement over the 96.76% return ratio that betting only pass gave us.

But is it?

Let's take a look. The single pass bets resulted in a loss of 72 units (2,220 x 3.24%). Pass bets with single odds bets would have given a loss of 96.60 units (3728 x 2.59% or 3728.00 – 3631.40). Placing single odds bets behind each pass point would have resulted in a loss that was 24.60 units greater than if we had limited ourselves to single pass bets with no odds backing them.

Backing our pass bets with double odds bets will increase our probability return ratio to 99.394%, but the same will be true in this case as for single odds; no less probability loss for more money risked. The total probability bet would be 4,620

units (1980 + 1320 + 1320) which, when multiplied by the loss ratio of 0.606%, will give a loss of the same 28 units.

Now let's look at what the results would have been had double odds bets been placed behind each pass point in the five casinos. The total bets for the 40 hours would have been $5,220. The total return would have been $5114.20. These would have given a return ratio of 97.97% (5114.20 ÷ 5220.00 x 100 = 97.97%). This is a better return ratio than the 97.41% for single odds, but the actual loss would have been 105.97 units (5,220 x 2.03% = 105.97 units), which is greater than the 96.60 units for the single odds, and 33.97 units greater loss than with no odds. This amounts to a 47% greater loss than with no odds.

Some experts instruct that each pass bet and come bet should be backed up with odds bets. Looking at the results from the five casinos, we can see that this obviously is not true for all pass and come bets. In a later chapter, I will show you when odds bets should be placed, and why they should be placed at only these times.

Odds bets by themselves give a probability return ratio percentage of 100. Therefore, they are, theoretically, not a probability percent factor as far as casino income is concerned. However, as we have shown, if the pass losses are greater than their 1.41% probability, the odds bets that were placed behind these additional pass losers would also become losers and would show up as an increased loss to that created by the pass bets alone.

Odds bets are not contract bets. They can be picked up at any time, and can be reinstated at any time. The house will call the odds bets that have been placed on come bets off on the coming out roll of a new pass point unless instructed to keep them working.

## FREE ODDS BETS ON DON'T PASS AND DON'T COME

After a point has been established by a coming out roll, if you are betting don't pass or don't come you can place an odds bet. In the case of the don't wagers, you must place a bet equal in size to the odds against the point number being rolled.

For example, if the point is 4 or 10 and your bet is one unit, you must place a bet of two units, for which you will win one unit if a 7 is rolled before a 4 or 10. If your point of 4 or 10 is rolled first, you will lose both your single don't pass bet and your two-unit odds bet, making your total loss three units.

If your don't pass point is 5 or 9, you must lay an odds bet of one and one-half units in order to have the opportunity of winning one unit. If you don't point is 6 or 8, you must lay an odds bet of ratio 6 to 5 in order to have a possible win of one unit. Consequently, in this case of the don't wagers—the same as with placing odds bets behind pass bets—you are restricted to unit bets of at least $5 (and multiples thereof) in order to be able to lay odds bets against all the points.

The return ratio for laying single odds on don't bets is 99.31 %. This is much higher than the 98.59 % return ratio for don't pass bets only, and also is a better return ratio than the 99.15% return ratio for the single odds bets for pass. However, when we consider the amounts bet in each case, 1,925 (1,980 minus 55 12's) for don't pass and 3,905 units for don't pass with single free odds, we get the same loss in each case (1,925 x 1.41% = 27 and 3,905 x 0.69 = 27). The only difference between the two cases has been the requirement for risking more than twice as much betting money with free odds than when betting don't pass only.

The return ratio for laying double odds on don't bets is 99.54%, a much more attractive figure than the 99.31% for laying single odds. However, when we consider that the amount bet when laying double odds is 5,885, we can compute the loss as 5,885 x 0.46% = 27, which is the same as for don't pass with no odds, as well as for don't pass with single odds. The only difference is that we must risk three times as much money as we risk for the no-odds bets!

The free odds are 100% return ratio bets. Therefore, they make no difference to the probability loss results whether they had or had not been placed. If there are more don't pass losers than the probability loss of 1.41% would create, the total loss for don't pass with odds would be increased over what don't pass would have produced alone. Also, if more don't pass wins occur than probability states there should be, don't pass bets with free odds would produce larger winnings or smaller losses than don't pass bets would have produced alone.

Don't pass and don't come bets and the free odds on them are not contract bets. These bets, or any part of them, can be taken off the table at any time. Naturally, since the return ratios for winning with the don't pass and don't come bets rise from a first-roll winning possibility of 55% return ratio to a return ratio possibility of 118.79% after a point has been established (plus the fact that the free odds probable return ratio is 100%), the casino is very willing to permit bettors to remove don't pass and don't come bets and all the bets related to them.

Usually, the only players that lay odds on don't pass and don't come bets are large bettors, those making $500 and $1,000 bets. If the bettor is betting the house limit on don't bets, he can increase the amount of his bet only by laying the odds on these bets. To bettors who place $2 and $5 bet, lay odds bets of $10 to win only $5 on a don't point of 4 or 10 appears to be a bad risk. They reason is that they could have accomplished the same win by betting only $5 more on the coming out bet instead of $10 more after the point has been established.

# B. SUCKER BETS

## THE FIELD BET

On each half of the casino crap table is a large, blocked area in which are printed seven numbers: 2, 3, 4, 9, 10, 11, 12. These are **field numbers**.

Sometimes a shooter will take a long time in completing his pass-point roll, maybe even 10 or 15 rolls. Since this can be very boring for the neophyte pass bettor, the casino offers him the **field**. This field is a delightful little place for him to spend his money in his spare time. It is a place where he can get action on every roll!

The temptation for making field bets is very great for the uninitiated. The field offers seven numbers, and should any of them appear on the next roll the bettor would win. If any one of the other four numbers 5, 6, 7, or 8 is rolled, he would lose. Seven numbers to four numbers looks pretty good, especially to the novice bettor, but this field is just another gimmick for enticing you to place more money on the table to increase the casino's income.

> Field bets are just another way the casino increases its income.

The basic odds of the field are very poor. Look at the following chart and you'll see what I mean.

| BASIC ODDS FOR FIELD BETS | | | |
|---|---|---|---|
| FIELD NUMBER | WAYS TO ROLL FIELD NUMBER | NON-FIELD NUMBER | WAYS TO ROLL NON-FIELD NUMBER |
| 2 | 1 | 5 | 4 |
| 3 | 2 | 6 | 5 |
| 4 | 3 | 7 | 6 |
| 9 | 4 | 8 | 5 |
| 10 | 3 | - | - |
| 11 | 2 | - | - |
| 12 | 1 | - | - |
| **Total** | **16** | | **20** |

This means that the odds against winning with a field bet are 20 to 16, and that the return ratio for these basic odds would be (16 + 16) ÷ (20 + 16) x 100 = 88.88%

Because of this poor return ratio, some casinos give double payouts on 2 and 12. This raises the field return to 18 and thus raises the return ratio to (16 + 18) ÷ (20 + 16) x 100 = 94.44% This is a great deal better than the 88.88% return ratio, but it is still far below the 98.59% return ratio for the pass and come bets.

Some casinos go further. They offer double returns on 2 and triple payouts on 12. This increases the field payout to 19 and raises the return ratio to 97.22%. However, pass, don't pass, come, and don't come at 98.59% return ratios are still much better bets.

Now let's compare actual results from the five casinos to the probability for the field.

| RESULTS COMPARED TO FIELD PROBABILITIES | | | | | | | |
|---|---|---|---|---|---|---|---|
| | SINGLE PAYOUT | | | DOUBLE 2 & DOUBLE 12 | | DOUBLE 2 & TRIPLE 12 | |
| | NON-FIELD ROLLS | FIELD PAYOUT | % RETURN | FIELD PAYOUT | % RETURN | FIELD PAYOUT | % RETURN |
| Frontier | 611 | 468 | 86.75% | 532 | 92.68% | 565 | 95.73% |
| Hilton | 491 | 439 | 94.41% | 503 | 101.29% | 533 | 104.62% |
| Caesars | 859 | 689 | 89.08% | 760 | 93.60% | 788 | 95.41% |
| Sands | 855 | 606 | 82.96% | 672 | 87.47% | 703 | 89.59% |
| Nugget | 1,439 | 1,197 | 90.82% | 1,324 | 95.64% | 1,384 | 97.91% |
| 40-Hours | 4,255 | 3,399 | 88.82% | 3,791 | 93.94% | 3,973 | 96.31% |
| Probability | 4,252 | 3,402 | 88.88% | 3,826 | 94.44% | 4,039 | 97.22% |

Once again the casino tables have performed closely to what the theoretical probabilities have dictated that they should.

The 96.31 % return for the five casinos if triple payouts for 12 had been paid might appear as not too bad when compared to the 96.76% return paid for the pass bets for the 40 hours at the five casinos. However, we must remember that when betting the field, a bet can be made on each roll of the dice. This means that 7,654 bets could have been made out of which 4,256 of them would have been losses and 3,399 of them would have been wins for a net loss of 282 units. This could also have been computed as 7,654 rolls of the dice multiplied by 3.69%.

When playing pass, a bet is made only for each coming out roll, which at the five casinos amounted to 2220 pass bet decisions consisting of 1,146 losses and 1,074 wins for a 72-unit loss.

At the Strip casinos where only double was paid for 12, the field loss would have been 464 units, 182 more than when triple was paid for 12. Theoretically, the field losses for 7,654 rolls would have been 213 units for triple 12 payouts (7654 x 2.78%), and 426 units for double 12 payouts (7654 x 5.56%),

and the loss would only have been 31 units for 2220 decisions at the theoretical pass return ratio of 98.59% (2220 x 1.41%).

The casinos know what they're doing when they offer the field, regardless of whether it offers a double 12 or a triple 12 payout. It knows that it will increase its income considerably even though the players only dabble in the field bets occasionally!

## ANY CRAPS

As the sophistication of a crap shooter increases, the size of his unit of betting often increases from the table minimums of $1 and $2 to the $5 and $25 chips—and after he has lost a few of these larger bets on the coming out roll because of craps, he begins to experiment with a bet that the dealers have been huckstering—any craps.

The **any craps** bet means that if any crap—2, 3 or 12—appears on the next roll, the bettor wins seven units for his one unit bet. The any crap bet is for one roll only. These casino hawkers advertise the any crap bet as being "insurance." Let's examine whom the insurance benefits.

Out of the 36 combinations of the dice, only four will produce craps (one for the 2, two for the 3, and one for the 12). This means that there are 32 dice combinations that will *not* produce a crap, thus making the odds 8 to 1 against rolling a crap on any roll. The casino table gives 7 to 1 odds for the any crap bet. It states this in its usual way as being "8 *for* 1" (7 to 1). As a result of the 7 to 1 odds, the any crap bets on the table will return 32 betting units for each 36 units that are bet, thus yielding a return ratio of 32/36 x 100 = 88.88%.

What is the justification for this so-called "insurance" that provides only an 88.88% return for protecting a 98.59% bet? Wouldn't the bettor be better off to place the money that he is betting on any craps as an addition to his pass bet at a 98.59% possible return ratio? Isn't a 98.59% possible return ratio a better risk than a possible 88.88% return ratio?

Quite often a dealer will practically demand $15 from a $100 pass bettor to "protect his bet"—and the sucker will give it to him!

If the bettor is willing to bet $115 on the coming out roll of the dice, which is what he is doing when he bets $15 on any craps and $100 on pass, it would be a better risk for him to bet the entire $115 to pass at a 98.59% possible return ratio rather than $15 of it at a possible return ratio of 88.88% and $100 of it at a possible return ratio of 98.59%. This should be obvious, but the dealer, a self-styled expert, has convinced the player otherwise.

Let's now compare the actual production of any crap rolls on the coming out rolls to the any crap probability.

| ACTUAL CRAP ROLLS COMPARED TO ANY CRAP PROBABILITY | | |
|---|---|---|
| | FIRST ROLL CRAPS | FIRST ROLL NON-CRAPS | RETURN RATIO |
| Frontier | 34 | 265 | 91.00% |
| Hilton | 22 | 212 | 75.21% |
| Caesars | 59 | 438 | 94.97% |
| Sands | 47 | 403 | 83.55% |
| Nugget | 76 | 664 | 82.16% |
| 40-Hours | 238 | 1,982 | 85.76% |
| Probability | 246.55 | 1,972.45 | 88.88% |

The performance of the dice confirm the probabilities, and they confirm that the any crap bet is not a very wise one. It is a sucker bet.

## 2, 3, AND 12

The casino table has a space at the middle where you can bet that the next roll can be any one of the three crap numbers. Very few bettors ever place bets on any of these individual crap numbers. The reason that these are unattractive is because most bettors are "pass-oriented." They think of winning only in relation to pass rolls and not in relation to betting on the don't pass options. As a result, crap number bets by the average bettor are considered only as insurance bets for protecting pass bets and not as the means for creating profits.

The any crap bet is more simple to execute than to attempt to guess which individual crap number might appear!

The odds against rolling a 2 or a 12 on any one roll are 35 to 1. The Strip casinos pay 29 to 1 odds, printed as "30 for 1" on their tables, and the Downtown casinos improve on this by offering 30 to 1 odds, printed as "31 for 1." Therefore, the return ratio for the 2 and 12 bets are 83.33% (30/36) for the Strip hotels and 86-11% (31/36) for the Downtown casinos.

The odds against rolling a 3 on a single roll are 17 to 1 (34 ways of no 3's and two ways for rolling a 3). Strip casinos pay 14 to 1 (stated as "15 for 1" on their tables). Downtown, the odds are 15 to 1 (printed "16 for 1" on their tables). These give a return ratio of 83.33% for the Strip and a return ratio of 88.88% for Downtown.

A pass bet could be "insured" by placing bets on all three of the individual crap numbers instead of placing a single bet on any craps. A $25 pass bet can be "insured" by placing a $4 bet on any craps where it would return $32 should any one of the three craps be rolled. Twenty-eight of these would be profit from the odds, and the other four would be a return of the bet. Instead of placing $4 on any crap, if $1 had been bet on 2 and $2 had been bet on 3 and $1 had been bet on 12, the $25 pass bet would also have been "insured."

At the Strip hotels, if a 2, 3 or 12 had been rolled, the return to the bettor would have been $30 in each case. Had these individual bets been made at a Downtown casino, the return would have been $31 for either a 2 or 12 and $32 for a 3. Consequently, if you feel that you should "insure" a pass bet, you should use the any crap bet where you would be assured a possible $32 return and have a simpler bet to place.

Let's now compare the actual production of 2, 12 and 3 on the coming out rolls at the five casinos to what the probabilities indicate that they should have been.

| ACTUAL CRAP ROLLS COMPARED TO THEIR PROBABILITIES | | | |
|---|---|---|---|
| | NO. OF 2'S 1ST ROLL | 30 FOR 1 RETURN RATIO | 31 FOR 1 RETURN RATIO |
| Frontier | 10 | 100.33% | 103.68% |
| Hilton | 4 | 51.28% | 52.99% |
| Caesars | 15 | 90.72% | 93.75% |
| Sands | 13 | 86.67% | 89.55% |
| Nugget | 18 | 72.98% | 75.41% |
| 40-Hours | 60 | 81.11% | 83.82% |
| Probability | 60½ | 83.33% | 86.11% |
| | NO. OF 12'S 1ST ROLL | 30 FOR 1 RETURN RATIO | 31 FOR 1 RETURN RATIO |
| Frontier | 6 | 60.20% | 62.21% |
| Hilton | 5 | 64.10% | 66.24% |
| Caesars | 9 | 54.43% | 56.25% |
| Sands | 7 | 46.67% | 48.22% |
| Nugget | 15 | 60.81% | 62.84% |
| 40-Hours | 42 | 56.78% | 58.72% |
| Probability | 60½ | 83.33% | 86.11% |

*(continued)*

| ACTUAL CRAP ROLLS COMPARED TO THEIR PROBABILITIES *(continued)* | | | |
|---|---|---|---|
| | NO. OF 3'S 1ST ROLL | 15 FOR 1 RETURN RATIO | 16 FOR 1 RETURN RATIO |
| Frontier | 18 | 90.30% | 96.32% |
| Hilton | 13 | 83.33% | 88.88% |
| Caesars | 35 | 105.85% | 112.90% |
| Sands | 27 | 90.00% | 96.00% |
| Nugget | 43 | 87.16% | 92.97% |
| 40 hours | 136 | 91.93% | 98.06% |
| Probability | 123 | 83.33% | 88.88% |

Very little can be deduced from these results except that sometimes the dice do and sometimes they don't!

We might attempt to conclude from the consistently poor returns for 12 that the dice are weighted so as to produce fewer of these numbers, but when we look back to page 28 we see that the dice produced a total of 2,505 single-die 6's when the probable number was 2551. This gave a 98.20% production, which indicates that the total number of the dice production of coming out 12's should have been much greater than the 42 which appeared on the coming out rolls.

## 11

Another popular coming out bet is 11. It is so popular that at times, bettors will call for it on rolls after a point has been established. Like craps and field, this bet is for just one roll of the dice.

The true odds for rolling an 11 with a single roll are 17 to 1, the same as for a 3 (34 ways for no 11 to two ways to roll 11). The Las Vegas Strip casinos pay 14 to 1 with the tables stating "15 for 1." The Downtown casinos pay 15 to 1, stating this as "16 for 1." As is the same for 3, the return ratio is 83.33% for uptown and 88.88% return ratio for downtown.

The following chart shows the results for coming out 11's for the five casinos.

| NUMBER OF 11'S COMING OUT ROLLS | | | |
|---|---|---|---|
| | NO. OF 11'S 1ST ROLL | 15 FOR 1 RETURN RATIO | 16 FOR 1 RETURN RATIO |
| **Frontier** | 14 | 70.23% | 74.88% |
| **Hilton** | 11 | 70.51% | 75.21% |
| **Caesars** | 29 | 87.70% | 93-55% |
| **Sands** | 17 | 56.67% | 60.44% |
| **Nugget** | 44 | 89.19% | 95-13% |
| **40-Hours** | 115 | 77.74% | 82.92% |
| **Probability** | 123 | 83.33% | 88.88% |

The actual production of 11 for the 7,654 rolls of the dice was 399. The probability was 425. Thus the production of 11's was 93.65% of what it should have been.

There were 2,219 coming out rolls of the dice, of which 115 were 11. The probable number for 2,219 rolls is 123. Thus the production of 11 for the coming out 11's was 93.49%, which, for all practical purposes, is the same as the 93.65% production of 11 for all the 7654 rolls of the dice. In the case of 11, the dice distributed themselves proportionately between coming out rolls and the other rolls.

When we look at the return ratios for rolling 11 and at those for pass and come, we can easily see that a bettor would have a better return if he were to place the bets that he is tempted to place on 11 on bets to pass or come at their 98.59% probability return ratios instead of at an 83.33% or 88.88% return ratio. It isn't as much fun, but it makes better sense.

> Betting pass or come isn't as exciting as betting 11, but it makes more sense. The key to beating the casino at craps is making good bets and staying away from sucker bets.

# 7

The game of craps is built around the 7. If you throw a 7 on the coming out roll, you win. If you roll a 7 on any other roll, you lose. No other dice number serves two purposes!

Since there are six combinations of the dice that can produce a 7, the odds against rolling a 7 on any single roll are 5 to 1 (30 dice combinations for not rolling a 7 to six combinations for rolling a 7). The casinos offer 4 to 1 odds against having a 7 rolled with a single roll. This results in a probable return ratio of 83.33%. Like other sucker bets, this one is described on the table as having a payout of "5 for 1."

If this bet were to be removed from the casino crap tables, it is doubtful if it would be missed. An 11 is much more exciting, and it gives a much greater unit payoff for a single unit bet.

Let's chart the 7 for coming out performance, the same as we have charted the other romantic single numbers and also so our records will be complete.

| NUMBER OF 7'S COMING OUT ROLLS | | |
|---|---|---|
| | NO. OF 7'S COMING OUT | RETURN RATIO |
| **Frontier** | 40 | 66.88% |
| **Hilton** | 25 | 53.42% |
| **Caesars** | 96 | 96.58% |
| **Sands** | 76 | 84.44% |
| **Nugget** | 120 | 81.08% |
| **40-Hours** | 357 | 80.45% |
| **Probability** | 370 | 83.33% |

The 7 is another example of where the dice performed closely to what probability dictated they should.

## 6 AND 8

At each end of the casino table on its front corners are two small adjoining squares. One is marked with a 6. The other is marked with an 8. A bet placed in either one of these boxes wagers that either a 6 or an 8 will be rolled *before* a 7 is rolled. These bets are not contract bets, so they can be picked up at any time.

These bets pay no odds. They are even-money bets, paying the same amount as you bet. Since there are six ways for rolling a 7 to five ways for rolling either a 6 or an 8, the odds against winning either of these bets is 6 to 5, which gives a return ratio of 90.91% (10 units returned for each 11 units bet).

The chart that follows shows how 6 and 8 bets would have performed at the five casinos. For these calculations we assume that bets would not have been placed on the coming out rolls and that they would have been placed with the second roll.

| NUMBER OF 6'S & 8'S COMING OUT ROLLS | | | | | |
|---|---|---|---|---|---|
| | NO. OF 6'S AFTER COME OUT | NO. OF 8'S AFTER COME OUT | NO. OF 7'S AFTER COME OUT | 6'S RETURN RATIO | 8'S RETURN RATIO |
| **Frontier** | 110 | 118 | 126 | 93.18% | 96.72% |
| **Hilton** | 89 | 104 | 102 | 93.18% | 100.97% |
| **Caesars** | 138 | 157 | 188 | 84.66% | 91.01% |
| **Sands** | 140 | 147 | 181 | 87.23% | 89.64% |
| **Nugget** | 259 | 255 | 311 | 90.88% | 90.11% |
| **40-Hours** | 736 | 781 | 908 | 89.54% | 92.48% |
| **Probability** | 755 | 755 | 906 | 90.91% | 90.91% |

The 6 and 8 bets are favored by some small bettors who, for some strange reason, feel that their opportunities for winning are greater with 90.91 % 6 and 8 bets than with 98.59% possible return-ratio come bets. The 6 and 8 bets are not contract bets, so they can be removed at any time.

## PLACE BETS

At the rear of each half of the crap table, stretching lengthwise, are six adjoining squares that are numbered 4, 5, 6, 8, 9, and 10. These squares are used for holding come bets and for indicating the pass point by having a marker placed on the square whose number is that of the pass point. These squares are also employed for holding place bets that are placed at the rear of the squares.

A place bet is a bet similar to the 6 and 8 bets. A bet placed on one of the numbers is a wager that that particular number will be rolled before a 7 is rolled. A place bet is not a contract bet, so it can be removed at any time. If a place-bet bettor calls "**down**," he wants his place bets picked up from the numbers and returned to him. If he calls "**off**", he wants his place bets left on their numbers, but after they have been called off, they are not wagers until he reinstates them by calling them working.

If a place bet number is rolled while his place bets are off, he would not be paid any winnings. A bettor may qualify his off call as "Off for the next roll" or "Off on the coming out," in which cases the place bets would be back in action on the roll that followed the off roll.

It is customary for the casino to handle all place bets as being off on the coming out of a new point. This happens when the roller has just made a pass by rolling his point at a time when there are place bets on the numbers. It would be very inconvenient and time consuming should all the place bets be removed at this time, only to be re-bet after a new coming out roll has established a new point. Also, if a bettor has his place bets removed at the completion of a winning point, he might not replace them, or probably not all of the amounts that were on them, after the dice have come out.

The odds on these bets favor the casino much more than pass and come bets. Consequently, it is to the casino's advantage to have these bets reinstated. Therefore, by automatically taking them off and then reinstating them, the casino acts in a way that will encourage you to keep your place bets working.

If you wish to have your place bets in effect on the coming out roll, you say, "Bets working on the come out," in which case a marker will be placed on one of your bets showing that they are all working.

A place bet pays odds. As a result, the minimum bet is $5 for place bets on 4, 5, 9, and 10; and the minimum bet is $6 for place bets on 6 and 8. Place bets in larger amounts are made up of multiples of these amounts. If a 4 or a 10 place bet becomes a winner, the winning amount is $9 for the $5 bet. The $9 is paid to the bettor, and his $5 place bet remains working on the number unless he calls it down or off. For a 5 or 9 place bet, the payout is $7 for the $5 bet. The payout is also $7 for the $6 place bets on 6 and 8.

Sometimes the place bets are romanticized by saying that a place bet is a combination of an even-money bet and an odds bet. The $5 place bets on 4 and 10 are said to consist of a $1 even-money bet and a $4 (quadruple) odds bet, thus making the payout consist of $1 for the even-money bet plus $8 for the odds (2 to 1) on the $4 bet. Likewise, the $5 place bets on 5 and 9 consist of a $1 even-money bet and a $4 (quadruple) odds bet, making a payout of $1 for the even-money bet and $6 for the odds (3 to 2) on the $4 odds bet. The 6 and 8 place bets consist of a $1 even bet plus a $5 (quintuple) odds bet, making a payout of $1 for the even-money bet plus $6 for the odds (6 to 5) on the $5 odds bet.

Whether the place bets are romanticized or not, the payouts are $9 for $5 bets on 4 and 10, $7 for $5 bets on 5 and 9, and $7 for $6 bets on 6 and 8.

Some casinos will permit smaller bets than $5. They will permit bets of $3 on 4 and 10 with a payout of $5. They will also permit $3 bets on 5 and 9 with rewards of $4. In larger casinos, $3 place bets on 6 and 8 pay only $3 winnings. In smaller casinos, where 50-cent chips are present, $3 place bets on 6 and 8 pay winnings of $3.50, which give them the same payout percent as the $7 that is paid for a $6 bet.

Let's now look at charts that show the probability return ratios for the various place bets.

## PROBABILITY RETURN RATIOS FOR PLACE BETS

| $5 PLACE BETS | | | | | |
|---|---|---|---|---|---|
| PLACE BET NUMBER | WINS | LOSSES | RETURN | AMOUNT BET | RETURN RATIO |
| 4 | 3 | 6 | 42 | 45 | 93.33% |
| 5 | 4 | 6 | 48 | 50 | 96.00% |
| 6 | 5 | 6 | 65 | 66 | 98.48% |
| 8 | 5 | 6 | 65 | 66 | 98.48% |
| 9 | 4 | 6 | 48 | 50 | 96.00% |
| 10 | 3 | 6 | 42 | 45 | 93.33% |
| Place Bets as a Group | | | 310 | 322 | 96.27% |

TRAP AND SUCKER BETS

| $3 PLACE BETS | | |
|---|---|---|
| RETURN | AMOUNT BET | RETURN RATIO |
| 24 | 27 | 88.88% |
| 28 | 30 | 93.33% |
| 30 | 33 | 90.91% (larger) |
| 32.50 | 33 | 98.48% (smaller) |
| 30 | 33 | 90.91% (larger) |
| 32.50 | 33 | 98.48% (smaller) |
| 28 | 30 | 93.33% |
| 24 | 27 | 88.88% |
| 164 | 180 | 91.11% (larger) |
| 169 | 180 | 94-44% (smaller) |

We can see from these charts that by lowering the place bet amounts to $3 that the odds favoring the casino have been increased. In the case of the 6 and 8, the payout to the casino has been increased from 1.52% to 9.19% in larger casinos because you will not receive any odds when betting 6 or 8.

Let's see what the difference would be in dollars between the casino's income from the $5 place bets and the $3 place bets.

## CASINO'S INCOME FROM $5 AND $3 PLACE BETS

| $5 PLACE BETS | | | |
|---|---|---|---|
| PLACE BET NUMBER | AMOUNT BET | CASINO PERCENT | CASINO INCOME |
| 4 | $45 | 6.67% | $3.00 |
| 5 | $50 | 4.00% | $2.00 |
| 6 | $66 | 1.52% | $1.00 |
| 8 | $66 | 1.52% | $1.00 |
| 9 | $50 | 4.00% | $2.00 |
| 10 | $45 | 6.67% | $3.00 |
| Totals | $322 | 3.73% | $12.00 |

| $3 PLACE BETS | | |
|---|---|---|
| **AMOUNT BET** | **CASINO PERCENT** | **CASINO INCOME** |
| $27 | 11.12% | $3.00 |
| $30 | 6.67% | $2.00 |
| $33 | 9.19% | $3.00 (larger) |
| $33 | 1.50% | $2.50 (smaller) |
| $33 | 9.19% | $3.00 (larger) |
| $33 | 1.50% | $2.50 (smaller) |
| $30 | 6.67% | $2.00 |
| $27 | 11.12% | $3.00 |
| $180 | 8.89% | $16.00 (larger) |
| $180 | 6.11% | $11.00 (smaller) |

By permitting $3 place bets, the larger casinos have increased their winnings from $12 to $16 (33.33%) with having less money bet ($180 bet with $3 place bets compared to $322 with $5 place bets), which is 44.12% less. By permitting $3 place bets, the casino is trying to look like Santa Claus to the small bettor by offering him a "big boy's" bet at a bargain price.

We must not forget that the casino will never voluntarily permit any bet that is not advantageous to it. If $3 place bets yielded better return ratios to the player than $5 ones, the casinos would not offer them. They would force the place-bet hopeful to extend himself to the $5 bets.

There is a class of crapshooters that finds the place bets very attractive. This group consists of the very large bettors who bet sums close to or equal to the casino's maximum. The place bets give these bettors the opportunity to wager total amounts at one time that are as large as six times the casino's limit by betting the

> Casinos will never willingly permit any bet that is not good for their profit picture.

maximum amount on each place bet number. The place bets not only give such bettors the opportunity to win large amounts quickly, but they also help them to lose large sums of money in a very short time.

## HARDWAY BETS

Another type of exciting bet on the crap table is the **hardway** bet. These are located in a little box at the middle of the table. In other boxes at the same location are the 11, any craps, individual craps bets, and 7—all advertising their shaded odds.

All you have to do to place a hardway bet is to throw your money toward the middle of the table and shout "Hardway 4!" or "hardway" any other number you want to bet. The stickman will be happy to place your money on its proper hardway number. All the other bets at this middle-table location can be made the same way with the stickman's assistance.

The hardway numbers are:

- 4 made with two 2's
- 6 made with two 3's
- 8 made with two 4's
- 10 made with two 5's

What makes these combinations be hardways is that there is only one position of the 36 combinations of the dice for each one of these hardway numbers. Consequently, the odds against having any one of these occur on any one roll are 35 to 1, the same as for the 2 and 12. However, the hardways are not played as one-roll bets, as are the 2 and 12. A hardway bet is a wager that the hardway number will be rolled *before* either a 7 or the same dice number (consisting of other dice combinations which add to the same total as the hardway number) is rolled.

There are three dice combinations that add up to 4, one of which is the hardway 2 and 2. There are six dice combinations that add up to 7. Consequently, there is one way of winning a hardway 4 and eight ways of losing it, thus making the odds 8 to 1 against winning with a hardway 4 bet. The same is true for the hardway 10 (5 and 5).

There are five dice combinations that add up to 6, one of which is the hardway 3 and 3. This leaves four other dice combinations that add up to 6 which, when added to the six combinations adding to 7, make 10 ways to lose the hardway 6 bet against the one way to win it. Therefore, the odds are 10 to 1 against winning with a hardway 6 bet. The same is also true for the hardway 8 (4 and 4).

The casino tables give odds for the hardway 4 and hardway 10 of "8 for 1," which we have learned means giving odds of 7 to 1. This results in an 88.88% return ratio for hardway 4 and hardway 10.

For the hardway 6 and hardway 8, casino tables show "10 for 1," thus giving 9 to 1 odds, and making the return ratios 90.91% for hardway 6 and hardway 8.

After a 4, 6, 8 or 10 has been established as a point, many bettors will place a hardway bet on the point number. The friendly crap table dealers also encourage these bets. Again, it is obvious that placing these same amounts of money as bets either as odds behind the pass bet (a 100% return ratio) or as a come bet (a 98.59% return ratio) would give much better probable returns—but uneducated bettors like what looks like getting paid large odds.

## UNDER 7 AND OVER 7

Some casinos have spaces served by the stickman at the middle of the table that are marked "Under 7" and "Over 7." A bet placed on the **Under 7** is a bet that the next roll of the dice will be a number that is less than 7. A bet placed on the **Over 7** is a bet that the next roll of the dice will produce a number greater than 7.

In both cases the bettor has 15 chances to win against 21 for losing. The probable return ratio is (15 + 15) ÷ (21 + 15) x 100 = 83.33%

## HORN BETS

Some casinos have a space marked "Horn" that is often embellished by a picture of the Horn of Plenty. The **horn** bet requires a minimum bet of $2. If a 2, 3, 11 or 12 appears on the next roll, the horn bettor wins. The amount of his payment depends upon which of the four numbers has been rolled, because the payout is made in the proportion of the table's payouts for 2, 3, 11 and 12. Actually the $2 minimum consists of an individual 50-cent bet on each of the numbers. Consequently, the return at smaller casinos will be $15.50 for a 2 or 12 (31 for 1) and $8 for a 3 or 11 (16 for 1).

Like all the other sucker bets, this bet has been added to the table strictly for the purpose of attracting suckers into betting more money so that the casino can profit more from its percentage advantage.

# SUMMARY OF CRAP TABLE BETS

Before studying the charts of the various bets that we have discussed in this chapter, we should examine one of the curious differences between betting pass and betting don't pass.

We have already showed that the basic odds for craps are 1,004 to 976 against making a pass, and 976 to 949 against winning with a don't pass bet. Both of these gave return ratios of 98.59% which translates into saying that when you bet either pass or don't pass, you will face the probability of losing $1.41 for each $100 that you wager.

However, this does not mean that you will lose the same amount of money for the same number of rolls of the dice on the crap table. Let's examine this concept.

If the dice are rolled enough times to conclude 1,980 points, the probability is that they will produce 1,004 losses and 976 wins for the bettor who bets pass, giving him a loss of 1,004 – 976 = 28 betting units. This could also be computed as 19.80 x 1.41 = 28 betting units. While these dice were being rolled for these 1,980 points, if you had been betting don't pass, you would not have been engaged in 1,980 win and lose decisions. You could have engaged in only 1,925 conclusive bets because 55 twelves would have appeared for no decisions. As a result, you would have lost only 27 betting units (976 – 949 or 19.25 x 1.41).

This difference between pass losses and don't pass losses has been pointed out so that when small differences appear between pass and don't pass results, they will not confuse you. This difference between 28 units loss for the pass, pass with single odds, and pass with double odds and the unit loss of only 27 for the comparable don't pass bets was also present in our discussion of odds bets.

In our tabulation we list the number of bets that probability says each type of bet could produce during 1,000 rolls of the dice. During these 1,000 rolls, the probability exists that there will be 298 coming out rolls. This would take about five hours. We next compute the total possible income for the casino (loss for the player) for each of these bets for both the Strip and Downtown by multiplying each bet's possible number of bets by the casino's income percent for each one.

We will assume that a minimum $1 bet is all that is required for all bets except place bets and odds bets. For place bets and odds bets, we will compute these casino incomes (bettor's losses) on the basis of $5 bets, the minimum that can be bet on these, to have every number pay its maximum casino payout. Craps 11, 2, 3, 12 and 7 will be computed as working only on the coming out roll. The field bet, place bets, and hardway bets will be computed as off on the coming out rolls and working on all other rolls, because this is the way these bets are normally played.

We will only compute the losses for the single odds bets because a bettor can only bet either single or double odds, not both of them at the same time. Also the loss for both is the same.

| | % RETURN | NUMBER OF BETS | STRIP $ LOST | DOWNTOWN $ LOST |
|---|---|---|---|---|
| **TOTAL POSSIBLE INCOME FOR THE CASINO ON ODDS BETS** | | | | |
| **Don't Pass w 2x Odds** | 99.54 | | | |
| **Pass w 2x Odds** | 99.39 | | | |
| **Don't Pass w 1x Odd** | 99.31 | 587.72 x 5 | 20 | 20 |
| **Don't Come w 1x Odds** | 99.31 | 1384.51 x 5 | 48 | 48 |
| **Pass w 1x Odds** | 99.15 | 496.66 x 5 | 21 | 21 |
| **Come w 1x Odds** | 99.15 | 1170.00 x 5 | 50 | 50 |
| **Don't Pass** | 98.59 | 289.72 | 4 | 4 |
| **Pass** | 98.59 | 298.00 | 4 | 4 |
| **Don't Come** | 98.59 | 682.00 | 10 | 10 |
| **Come** | 98.59 | 702.00 | 10 | 10 |
| **Place Bet 6** | 98.48 | 214.50 x 6 | 20 | 20 |
| **Place Bet 8** | 98.48 | 214.50 x 6 | 20 | 20 |
| **Field (2x 2; 3x 12)** | 97.22 | 702.00 | | 20 |
| **Place Bet 5** | 96.00 | 195.00 x 5 | 39 | 39 |
| **Place Bet 9** | 96.00 | 195.00 x 5 | 39 | 39 |
| **Field (2x 2; 2x 12)** | 94.44 | 702.00 | 39 | |
| **Place Bet 4** | 93.33 | 175.50 x 5 | 59 | 59 |
| **Place Bet 10** | 93.33 | 175.50 x 5 | 59 | 59 |
| **6** | 90.91 | 214.50 | 20 | 20 |
| **8** | 90.91 | 214.50 | 20 | 20 |
| **Hardway 6** | 90.91 | 214.50 | 20 | 20 |
| **Hardway 8** | 90.91 | 214.50 | 20 | 20 |
| **Hardway 4** | 88.88 | 175.50 | 20 | 20 |

*(continued)*

| TOTAL POSSIBLE INCOME FOR THE CASINO ON ODDS BETS *(continued)* | | | | |
|---|---|---|---|---|
| | % RETURN | NUMBER OF BETS | STRIP $ LOST | DOWNTOWN $ LOST |
| Hardway 10 | 88.88 | 175.50 | 20 | 20 |
| Any Crap | 88.88 | 298.00 | 33 | 33 |
| 11 (16 for 1) | 88.88 | 298.00 | | 33 |
| 3 (16 for 1) | 88.88 | 298.00 | | 33 |
| 2 (31 for 1) | 86.11 | 298.00 | | 41 |
| 12 (31 for 1) | 86.11 | 298.00 | | 41 |
| 11 (15 for 1) | 83.33 | 298.00 | 50 | |
| 3 (15 for 1) | 83.33 | 298.00 | 50 | |
| 2 (30 for 1) | 83.33 | 298.00 | 50 | |
| 12 (30 for 1) | 83.33 | 298.00 | 50 | |
| 7 (5 for 1) | 83.33 | 298.00 | 50 | 50 |
| Under 7 (1 for 1) | 83.33 | 702.00 | 117 | 117 |
| Over 7 (1 for 1) | 83.33 | 702.00 | 117 | 117 |
| Totals* | | | $1,071 | $1,000 |

*In the totals, the pass and don't pass of $4 loss for each were not included because a player would not place separate bets for pass and don't pass and for pass with odds and don't pass with lay-up odds

Horn bets are not considered in the totals because these are the same as individual bets on 2, 3, 11, and 12. A bettor would not repeat these.

The dollar amounts were not recorded as decimal fractions but were stated at their nearest whole numbers. This leads to some minor discrepancies. For example, the loss for pass with odds is shown as $21, and the loss for the pass alone is shown as $4. Since the only difference between these loses is that $5 would have been bet instead of $1 when an odds bet was placed to back a pass bet, we would have expected a loss of $20 instead of $21. The actual mathematical value for pass (1.41% x 298) was $4.20, which when multiplied by 5 would have equaled $21. This $4 instead of $4.20 makes no real difference since the tabulation is intended only as giving a visual picture of potential loss distribution.

It is very unlikely that any player would ever indulge himself to the extent of making bets on every bet offered on a crap table. If he were betting pass, he certainly would not bet don't pass at the same time. It is, however, very common practice for bettors to bet both 11 and any craps on the same coming out roll.

## WHAT DO THESE POSSIBLE LOSSES TELL US?

What these total possible losses tell us is that there are many ways on the crap table for a player to part with his money. From the large losses that speculation with trap and sucker bets can create, it is obvious that when betting only the minimum amounts, you can hurt yourself much more than you wish by just dabbling in some of these bets. Of course, you can never dabble in them enough to satisfy the casino's insatiable appetite for your money!

There is, however, a great difference between a potential loss of $1,000 that could be created by minimum bets on all the bets offered by the crap table, and the $4 potential loss with only pass or don't pass bets with the minimum size of bets.

> Every bet on the casino crap table is a separate bet. Treat your wagers this way, staying with the best bets.

Never lose sight of the fact every bet on the casino table is a separate bet. Its odds depend upon its relationship to the 36 positions of the dice and to the particular conditions that limit its betting boundaries.

For example, early in this chapter we developed return ratios of 99.15% for pass with odds and 99.31 % for don't pass with **lay-up odds**, and we treated the odds bets with their parent bets as though the combination of the two bets were a single bet. Regardless of intent, this is not true when the *first bet* is made. The odds bet and the pass bet are two separate bets. The same is true for don't pass and the free odds bets placed on them.

It is necessary for you to have placed a pass or a come bet before you are permitted to place an odds bet, but the size of your pass or come bet does not determine the size of your odds bet. Your odds bet can be the same size as your pass or come bet. It can be larger, up to twice as large in some casinos (even up to triple or 100x sometimes), or it can be less than the size of your pass or come bet. All of these odds bets would be paid winnings in proportion to the correct odds for them, not in accordance to the size of the original pass or come bets.

An odds bet cannot be made unless a point has been established, and therefore, it appears logical that the effect of the odds bet should be considered as a part of the overall payout, yet we cannot discard the fact that twelve of the coming out rolls (six for 7, two for 11, and four for craps) will decide part of the return ratio without any assist from an odds bet.

Secondly, we must consider that the only time when the pass return ratio is 98.59% is when the dice first come out. After a point has been established the potential pass payout percent drops. For a 4 or a 10 it becomes 66.67%. For a 5 or a 9, it becomes 80.00%. And for a 6 or an 8, it becomes 90.91%. The odds bets always remain 100% probability return ratio regardless of when they are placed.

Casinos have introduced all the bets discussed in this chapter for just one purpose: To attract players into betting more money. Gambling casinos operate numbers games. They collect a percentage of all money wagered as profit. Consequently, the more opportunities casinos offer for betting, the more money will be bet, thus increasing casinos' profits.

# TRAP AND SUCKER BETS

> Casinos could not afford to offer crap games if the only bets they offered were pass and don't pass. Hint: Stay away from the sucker bets.

The bets described in this chapter are not expected to be the only bets that will be offered forever on casino crap tables. Others will be conceived in the future, all for one purpose—to attract more betting. The Under 7 and Over 7 bets at even money, yield only an 83.33% return ratio, so why not a bet at a 5 for 1 payout for the next roll being a 4 or under, or for the next roll being a 10 or higher? This would yield a 83.33% return ratio, the same as the under and over bets—and also the same as the 83.33% return ratio for the popular 11 bet.

If 11 can attract suckers, so can other bets at the same poor return ratio!

Now, let's look at the fallacies of craps, where all your dreams can come true if you get lucky—though more than likely, your dreams will become financial nightmares!

 **EXPOSING THE FALLACIES**

All crap addicts live in Fantasyland. Let one of them hear that a friend is going to Las Vegas and he gives him $5 and says, "When you get to the casino, go straight to the crap table, and regardless what is happening, place the $5 immediately on hardway 8. If it wins, let it ride, and if it wins again, pick up the money for me."

This addict is admitting several things. First, he can't resist betting on craps even if he's not physically where the action is.

Second, he fantasizes that the opportunity to win $500 with a $5 bet exists exactly at a particular moment he's chosen in time. He most likely admits to himself that if he were there, he'd probably chicken out and pick up his $50 after the first hardway 8. The odds also favor his placing only a $1 bet instead of a $5 bet. But by having his friend bet for him, he can only lose $5, whereas if he were there in person, he would lose much more than $5 during an evening's play. By giving the $5 to his friend with firm betting instructions, he eliminates any chance of upsetting his fantasy.

Finally, he has already fantasized how to spend the $500. He probably would finance himself on a trip to Las Vegas. Since his luck has been so good because of this fantasized $500 win, he dreams that he would eventually win a fortune. He will fantasize this result long before he has won even the first leg of his $500 dream!

How many times has each of us fantasized placing a $1 bet on 2 and then leaving our bet to multiply while three consecutive 2's are rolled for a payout of $27,000? Many crap players have dreamed this, although most of them have yet to place their first $1 bet on 2! Have you ever dreamed of leaving the crap table to go to the men's room and accidentally leaving a bet on the table which, while you were absent, keeps multiplying and multiplying to the point where the dealer must remove your winnings after each roll because your bet has reached the table limit—and when you return, he gives you $10,000!

We've all had these fantasies, and none represent any actions that would be impossible to happen. At some time every day, at every crap table, doubling on the hardway 8 would be successful. Actually it should happen several times during the day. A triple run of 2's might occur once every several months.

As for having a small bet multiply through successive passes until the table maximum has been reached, thus forcing the removal of the winning amount on each successive pass, remember that at the Desert Inn, a crap shooter once rolled 26 consecutive passes! The unusual part about this spectacular performance was that not one of the passes thrown was a 7. If we spend twenty-four hours a day at a crap table for the next 3,000 years, we *may* see this happen again. Nothing is impossible!

All get-rich betting fantasies are founded on the rapid parlaying of bets. In other words, hot streaks originate upon having some particular bet repeat itself without the interference of a losing roll of a 7 or some other losing dice combination. This mind-boggling growth of winnings that such parlaying offers is what makes "Fantasy betting" schemes so attractive.

Most betting systems people dream up, whether quick-rich or slow-rich, involve consecutive occurrences. Some bettors will wait until two or three consecutive 7's have been rolled before making a place bet. Some bettors will make place bets with the intention of letting them remain for a certain number of rolls, hoping these rolls will be non-7's. Some bettors place field bets only after a certain number of consecutive non-field rolls have happened. All of us instinctively recognize that in order for our betting schemes to have reasonable chances to succeed, we must have projected at least a few consecutive occurrences into them.

In this chapter we develop probabilities for bets offered on the crap table to occur consecutively, and compare these with the actual performances for the 40 hours at the five casinos.

The next chart shows tabulations of what the probable results should be if we let pass and don't pass bets multiply. For calculating these, we employed 976 passes, 1,004 pass losses, 949 don't pass wins totaling 1,980 pass bet decisions with single-unit bets.

Multiplying factors on these tabulations were arrived at in the following way: If, for example, we should let a one-unit bet double (have nothing removed until after a second consecutive winning decision), we would have four units on the table after the second consecutive winning decision. If we then remove three units and return to our bet of one unit and if the next decision is a loss, we would have a return of only three units— the three we removed after the second consecutive decision.

On the other hand, if after we removed the three units, had the one unit we left been again multiplied by two consecutive winning decisions, we would have been able to remove another three units. Therefore, four consecutive wins would have a multiplying factor of 6 when we are permitting our bets to multiply through two consecutive winning decisions before removing any part of the bets; six consecutive wins would give a multiplying factor of 9 and so on.

If we were to leave our unit bets until they had multiplied through four consecutive winning decisions before removing any winnings, the multiplying factor would be 15, and it would increase by 15 for each four additional consecutive winning decisions.

The tabulations show what the probability results would be if each time we placed a unit bet, we would not remove our winnings above this unit until after some number (selected by us) of consecutive winning decisions had been rolled. After each loss, we would place a new unit bet at the next coming out roll. An examination of these tabulations shows that attempting to have every pass and don't pass bet multiply, even as much as seven times, involves less risk than betting on most of the trap and sucker bets. However, the returns on all bet multiplications will each be less than a single bet on pass or don't pass.

Permitting a bet to parlay does not constitute making a new bet with new money each time the dice come out. Not picking up the winnings from a pass or don't pass bet and then having this larger bet lose on the next point does not increase the loss. The loss is still the one unit with which the betting series began.

## CONSECUTIVE PASS WINS

| Consecutive Pass Category | Quantity In Each Category | Mult. Factor | Profit for Unit Bet | Mult. Factor | Profit 2 Consec. Wins | Mult. Factor | Profit 3 Consec. Wins | Mult. Factor | Profit 4 Consec. Wins | Mult. Factor | Profit 5 Consec. Wins | Mult. Factor | Profit 6 Consec. Wins | Mult. Factor | Profit 7 Consec. Wins | Mult. Factor | Profit 8 Consec. Wins | Mult. Factor | Profit 9 Consec. Wins | Mult. Factor | Profit 10 Consec. Wins |
|---|---|---|---|---|---|---|---|---|---|---|---|---|---|---|---|---|---|---|---|---|---|
| 1 | 252.2960 | 1 | 252.2960 | | | | | | | | | | | | | | | | | | |
| 2 | 124.3424 | 2 | 248.6848 | 3 | 373.0272 | | | | | | | | | | | | | | | | |
| 3 | 61.2928 | 3 | 183.8784 | 3 | 183.8784 | 7 | 429.0496 | | | | | | | | | | | | | | |
| 4 | 30.2072 | 4 | 120.8288 | 6 | 181.2432 | 7 | 211.4504 | 15 | 453.1080 | | | | | | | | | | | | |
| 5 | 14.8937 | 5 | 74.4685 | 6 | 89.3622 | 7 | 104.2559 | 15 | 223.4055 | 31 | 461.7047 | | | | | | | | | | |
| 6 | 7.3363 | 6 | 44.0178 | 9 | 66.0267 | 14 | 102.7082 | 15 | 110.0445 | 31 | 227.4253 | 63 | 462.1859 | | | | | | | | |
| 7 | 3.6251 | 7 | 25.3757 | 9 | 32.6259 | 14 | 50.7514 | 15 | 54.3765 | 31 | 112.3781 | 63 | 228.3813 | 127 | 460.3877 | | | | | | |
| 8 | 1.7813 | 8 | 14.2504 | 12 | 21.3756 | 14 | 24.9382 | 30 | 53.4390 | 31 | 55.2203 | 63 | 112.2219 | 127 | 226.2251 | 255 | 454.2315 | | | | |
| 9 | 0.8784 | 9 | 7.9056 | 12 | 10.5408 | 21 | 18.4464 | 30 | 26.3520 | 31 | 27.2304 | 63 | 55.3332 | 127 | 111.5568 | 255 | 223.3920 | 511 | 448.8624 | | |
| 10 | 0.4294 | 10 | 4.2940 | 15 | 6.4410 | 21 | 9.0174 | 30 | 12.8820 | 62 | 26.6228 | 63 | 27.0522 | 127 | 54.5338 | 255 | 109.4970 | 511 | 219.4234 | 1023 | 439.2762 |
| Totals | | | 976.0000 | | 964.5210 | | 950.6175 | | 933.6075 | | 910.5816 | | 885.1815 | | 852.7054 | | 787.7205 | | 668.2858 | | 439.2762 |
| ReturnRatio | | | 98.59% | | 97.95% | | 97.31% | | 96.44% | | 95.28% | | 94.00% | | 92.36% | | 89.08% | | 83.04% | | 71.48% |

## CONSECUTIVE DON'T PASS WINS

| Consecutive Pass Category | Quantity In Each Category | Mult. Factor | Profit for Wins | Mult. Factor | Profit 2 Consec. Wins | Mult. Factor | Profit 3 Consec. Wins | Mult. Factor | Profit 4 Consec. Wins | Mult. Factor | Profit 5 Consec. Wins | Mult. Factor | Profit 6 Consec. Wins | Mult. Factor | Profit 7 Consec. Wins | Mult. Factor | Profit 8 Consec. Wins | Mult. Factor | Profit 9 Consec. Wins | Mult. Factor | Profit 10 Consec. Wins |
|---|---|---|---|---|---|---|---|---|---|---|---|---|---|---|---|---|---|---|---|---|---|
| 1 | 245.5756 | 1 | 245.5756 | | | | | | | | | | | | | | | | | | |
| 2 | 121.0895 | 2 | 242.1790 | 3 | 363.2685 | | | | | | | | | | | | | | | | |
| 3 | 59.6961 | 3 | 179.0883 | 3 | 179.0883 | 7 | 417.8727 | | | | | | | | | | | | | | |
| 4 | 29.4347 | 4 | 117.7388 | 6 | 176.6082 | 7 | 206.0429 | 15 | 441.5205 | | | | | | | | | | | | |
| 5 | 14.4975 | 5 | 72.4875 | 6 | 86.9850 | 7 | 101.4825 | 15 | 217.4625 | 31 | 449.4225 | | | | | | | | | | |
| 6 | 7.1546 | 6 | 42.9276 | 9 | 64.3914 | 14 | 100.1644 | 15 | 107.3190 | 31 | 221.7926 | 63 | 450.7398 | | | | | | | | |
| 7 | 3.5243 | 7 | 24.6701 | 9 | 31.7187 | 14 | 49.3402 | 15 | 52.8645 | 31 | 109.2533 | 63 | 222.0309 | 127 | 447.5861 | | | | | | |
| 8 | 1.7412 | 8 | 13.9296 | 12 | 20.8944 | 14 | 24.3768 | 30 | 52.2360 | 31 | 53.9772 | 63 | 109.6959 | 127 | 221.1324 | 255 | 444.0060 | | | | |
| 9 | 0.8535 | 9 | 7.6815 | 12 | 10.2420 | 21 | 17.9235 | 30 | 25.6050 | 31 | 26.4585 | 63 | 53.7705 | 127 | 108.3945 | 255 | 217.6425 | 511 | 436.1385 | | |
| 10 | 0.2722 | 10 | 2.7220 | 15 | 4.0830 | 21 | 5.7162 | 30 | 8.1660 | 62 | 16.8764 | 63 | 17.1486 | 127 | 34.5694 | 255 | 69.4110 | 511 | 139.0942 | 1023 | 278.4606 |
| Totals | | | 949.0000 | | 937.2795 | | 922.9192 | | 905.1735 | | 877.7805 | | 853.3854 | | 811.6824 | | 731.0595 | | 575.2327 | | 278.4606 |
| ReturnRatio | | | 98.59% | | 97.99% | | 97.24% | | 96.32% | | 94.90% | | 93.63% | | 91.46% | | 87.27% | | 79.18% | | 63.76% |

Now let's see how the actual performance for consecutive decisions from the five casinos would have compared to what probability indicates they should have been:

| ACTUAL CONSECUTIVE PASSES | | | | | | | | | | |
|---|---|---|---|---|---|---|---|---|---|---|
| | 1 | 2 | 3 | 4 | 5 | 6 | 7 | 8 | 9 | 10 |
| **Frontier** | 36 | 24 | 7 | 1 | 6 | 0 | 0 | 0 | 0 | 0 |
| **Hilton** | 26 | 18 | 6 | 4 | 0 | 0 | 2 | 0 | 0 | 0 |
| **Caesars** | 58 | 30 | 14 | 13 | 3 | 0 | 1 | 2 | 0 | 0 |
| **Sands** | 52 | 25 | 20 | 9 | 3 | 0 | 0 | 1 | 0 | 0 |
| **Nugget** | 90 | 35 | 19 | 18 | 4 | 2 | 1 | 3 | 0 | 0 |
| **40-Hour Total** | 262 | 132 | 66 | 45 | 16 | 2 | 4 | 6 | 0 | 0 |
| **Probability** | 283 | 139 | 69 | 34 | 17 | 8 | 4 | 2 | 1 | ½ |

| ACTUAL CONSECUTIVE DON'T PASSES | | | | | | | | | | | | | | | |
|---|---|---|---|---|---|---|---|---|---|---|---|---|---|---|---|
| | 1 | 2 | 3 | 4 | 5 | 6 | 7 | 8 | 9 | 10 | 11 | 12 | 13 | 14 | 15 | 16 |
| **Frontier** | 32 | 19 | 9 | 5 | 3 | 1 | 0 | 0 | 0 | 0 | 0 | 0 | 0 | 0 | 0 | 1 |
| **Hilton** | 25 | 13 | 11 | 4 | 2 | 0 | 0 | 0 | 1 | 0 | 0 | 0 | 0 | 0 | 0 | 0 |
| **Caesars** | 63 | 29 | 15 | 5 | 5 | 2 | 1 | 1 | 0 | 0 | 0 | 0 | 0 | 0 | 0 | 0 |
| **Sands** | 48 | 29 | 13 | 10 | 5 | 2 | 0 | 0 | 0 | 0 | 0 | 0 | 0 | 0 | 0 | 0 |
| **Nugget** | 86 | 33 | 21 | 15 | 5 | 4 | 2 | 2 | 1 | 1 | 0 | 0 | 0 | 0 | 0 | 0 |
| **40-Hour Total** | 254 | 123 | 69 | 49 | 20 | 9 | 3 | 3 | 2 | 1 | 0 | 0 | 0 | 0 | 0 | 1 |
| **Probability** | 275 | 135 | 67 | 33 | 16 | 8 | 4 | 2 | 1 | ¼ | 0 | 0 | 0 | 0 | 0 | 0 |

We can see from these charts that the dice performed closely to their probability expectations except for one event. The lone exception was 16 consecutive don't pass decisions at the Frontier.

In examining the date for these 16 consecutive don't pass decisions, there is nothing unusual since the probability is that a crap should appear once during each nine rolls; therefore, two craps in 16 coming out rolls cannot be considered abnormal.

The unusual thing was that 16 don't pass decisions appeared in succession. If a crap table were to operate twenty-four hours a day with the dice being constantly rolled, the probability that 16 consecutive don't pass decisions would happen would be once in about six months. The fact it happened while the data for this book was being recorded was unusual but not improbable. The crap table at which this occurred had been in operation for much, much longer than six months. This 16 consecutive don't pass decision sequence was probably the completion of some past probability obligation.

The experience of having these 16 consecutive don't pass decisions occur was very informative. Not one person at the table, including the "friendly expert" dealers commented about it while it was happening. There was no excitement! No one was interested enough to keep count. If this had been the reverse and the dice had been performing with a run of 16 consecutive passes, the cheering and excitement would have been enormous. Sucker betting would have been huge, and the table would have been packed with smiling players.

## CRAP BETTORS ARE PASS-ORIENTED

Bettors at crap tables are "pass-oriented." Bets offered by the table make it this way. There are no sucker bets for the don't bettor. His only opportunities are don't pass and don't come. He has no side bets with which to pass the time when a shooter is engaged in a long decision. He could experiment with various crap bets, but a player sees these as "insurance" bets and not sources for profit. The crap table layout advertises winning with winning dice, not winning with losing dice.

Repeat, the table is pass-oriented!

While the 16 consecutive don't pass decisions were being rolled, I was recording each roll of the dice, and betting don't pass with each coming out roll. Even as I was betting don't pass and winning on each decision, I was not aware of what I was witnessing at the time. I did not realize what had happened until later when I was cataloguing and analyzing the data. I too had become pass-oriented through the years!

Prior to collecting my data for this book, I had computed the basic odds of the game and had confirmed them with articles written about craps. I decided on making minimum bets on don't pass for the simple reason that I would not have any tempting sucker bets in my same betting direction to lure me during long, boring point decisions. After all, my purpose for going to the crap tables was collecting data, not winning bets.

Only once during the 40 hours did I change my betting direction from don't pass to pass. That was at the Nugget when the table went empty except for me and one other player who refused to roll the dice. Because I was weary after collecting data and did not wish to see the action at the table stop, I rolled the dice for several hands, during which time the dice very kindly gave me winnings. My dice rolling attracted players, and I returned to my don't pass betting.

## THE FIELD OF FANTASIES

The field is also an area around which many fantasies have been created. The most fundamental fallacy is that if a bettor doubles his bet each time he loses, eventually he will win one unit when a field number is rolled. And if the field number is a 2 or a 12 (which it should be once in each 18 rolls), and if one of these appears with a high-money bet, the payoff will be enormous. This is the exciting possibility.

Another popular fantasy occurs later when the dreamer finds time somewhere in his gambling career to try the doubling scheme, or calculate its possibilities by counting on his fingers with each consecutive non-field roll until he learns that nine or ten consecutive non-field rolls can happen. This knowledge promotes his next field winning scheme. Here the bettor does not place a field bet until after a specific number of consecutive non-field numbers have been rolled (usually three, four, or five). If his bets continue to lose, he increases each by a single unit for a limited number of times or until he wins. Then he begins again, waiting for his selected number of consecutive non-field numbers to occur before repeating his betting cycle.

The latter fantasy is often promoted as a phenomenon that some dreamer has witnessed. It is usually told as an operation that had been engaged in by several partners making large bets, taking turns at the table to avoid missing even one roll of the dice. Sometimes the fantasy streak went on for days, with winnings growing to untold thousands of dollars. In fact, the money mountain became so large the casino resorted to threatening their lives if they ever returned! Naturally, the casino denied that it ever took place because, the dreamer explains, if word got out, everyone would bet this way and all casinos would go broke.

The following tabulations show how the consecutive probabilities compare to the actual field performances for the 7,654 rolls of the dice in the five casinos.

## FIELD

| CONSECUTIVE ROLL CATEGORIES | | | | | | | | | | | | | | | |
|---|---|---|---|---|---|---|---|---|---|---|---|---|---|---|---|
| | 1 | 2 | 3 | 4 | 5 | 6 | 7 | 8 | 9 | 10 | 11 | 12 | 13 | 14 | 15 | TOTAL ROLLS OF DICE |
| Frontier | 143 | 59 | 36 | 14 | 5 | 3 | | | | | | | | | | 468 |
| Hilton | 124 | 54 | 34 | 13 | 7 | 3 | | | | | | | | | | 439 |
| Caesars | 204 | 98 | 36 | 19 | 8 | 3 | 4 | 1 | 0 | 0 | 1 | | | | | 689 |
| Sands | 190 | 92 | 40 | 11 | 6 | 4 | 2 | | | | | | | | | 606 |
| Nugget | 338 | 171 | 77 | 37 | 12 | 5 | 3 | 1 | 1 | 1 | | | | | | 1,197 |
| Total | 999 | 474 | 223 | 94 | 38 | 18 | 9 | 2 | 1 | 1 | 1 | | | | | 3,399 |
| Probability | 1,050 | 467 | 207 | 92¼ | 41 | 18 | 8 | 3½ | 1 | ¾ | ½ | ½ | | | | 3,399 |

## NON-FIELD

| CONSECUTIVE ROLL CATEGORIES | | | | | | | | | | | | | | | |
|---|---|---|---|---|---|---|---|---|---|---|---|---|---|---|---|
| | 1 | 2 | 3 | 4 | 5 | 6 | 7 | 8 | 9 | 10 | 11 | 12 | 13 | 14 | 15 | TOTAL ROLLS OF DICE |
| Frontier | 6 | 69 | 44 | 30 | 12 | 4 | 1 | 2 | 2 | | | | | | | 611 |
| Hilton | 108 | 69 | 32 | 7 | 10 | 4 | 4 | 0 | 1 | 1 | | | | | | 491 |
| Caesars | 160 | 103 | 42 | 32 | 14 | 8 | 7 | 4 | 2 | 1 | 0 | 1 | | | | 859 |
| Sands | 143 | 82 | 48 | 35 | 12 | 9 | 7 | 1 | 5 | 2 | 0 | 0 | 1 | 0 | 1 | 855 |
| Nugget | 281 | 158 | 98 | 85 | 23 | 10 | 11 | 3 | 1 | 2 | 1 | | | | | 1,439 |
| Total | 788 | 481 | 264 | 162 | 71 | 35 | 30 | 10 | 11 | 6 | 1 | 1 | 1 | 0 | 1 | 4,255 |
| Probability | 840 | 467 | 259 | 144 | 81 | 44½ | 24½ | 14½ | 7½ | 4¼ | 2¼ | 1¼ | ¾ | ³/₈ | ¼ | 4,255 |

If we examined all the possibilities for employing field numbers, we would fill volumes of notebooks with calculations. In the end we would conclude that none of these schemes would produce a system that would consistently win. If there were such a system, someone would have already discovered it and all casinos would be in serious trouble.

# DOUBLING THE BET SIZE AFTER EVERY LOSING BET

The only betting system that might even possibly be considered foolproof is the one where the bettor doubles his bet every time he loses. However, this system requires two conditions: that no table limit exists, and that the bettor has unlimited funds. The following chart shows the total funds needed for such a betting performance in the five casinos, assuming only a $1 unit bet.

| TOTAL FUNDS NEEDED TO DOUBLE A BET EVERY TIME YOU LOSE | | | |
|---|---|---|---|
| NUMBER OF PRIOR CONSECUTIVE NON-FIELD BETS | AMOUNT BET ON PRIOR ROLLS ($) | AMOUNT BET ON CURRENT ROLL ($) | TOTAL BANKROLL REQUIRED FOR WINNING $1 |
| 0 | 0 | 1 | 1 |
| 1 | 1 | 2 | 3 |
| 2 | 3 | 4 | 7 |
| 3 | 7 | 8 | 15 |
| 4 | 15 | 16 | 31 |
| 5 | 31 | 32 | 63 |
| 6 | 63 | 64 | 127 |
| 7 | 127 | 128 | 255 |
| 8 | 255 | 256 | 511 |
| 9 | 511 | 512 | 1,023 |
| 10 | 1,023 | 1,024 | 2,047 |
| 11 | 2,047 | 2,048 | 4,095 |
| 12 | 4,095 | 4,096 | 8,191 |
| 13 | 8,191 | 8,192 | 16,383 |
| 14 | 16,383 | 16,384 | 32,767 |
| 15 | 32,767 | 32,768 | 65,535 |
| 16 | 65,535 | 65,536 | 131,071 |

We can see now why the casino places an upper limit on betting. It prevents success with any doubling scheme, whether with the field or with some other bet. For example, if you had been doubling your losing bets when you were betting pass at the Frontier with a $1 unit when the 16 consecutive losing rolls occurred, you would have needed a bankroll of $131,071 to have survived long enough to place a winning bet on the 17th coming out roll—just to have salvaged a $1 win!

Also remember that raising the minimum betting limit works against the parlaying scheme. An increase in the minimum bet from $1 to $2 would have increased the field bankroll for covering the one case of 15 consecutive non-field rolls to $131,071 and the pass bankroll at the Frontier to $262,143.

Actually, the minimum bets at both the Sands where the 15 consecutive non-field rolls happened and at the Frontier where the 16 consecutive loss rolls took place had minimum bets of $2. Therefore, the actual bankrolls that would have been required at both casinos for winning a minimum bet of $2 would have been $131,071 at the Sands and $262,143 at the Frontier, assuming, of course, that there were no maximum limits at either casino.

Many casinos have minimum bets of $2 at their crap tables, and there are many that have $5 minimums. When studying any gambling scheme, never lose sight of the fact that the casino can change its minimum and maximum limits anytime that it feels threatened by any betting system.

# ANY CRAPS

The any crap bet is used primarily for "insurance" reasons. With its 88.88% return ratio, it is poor insurance, but people who distrust their own judgment will probably always find the any crap insurance bet attractive.

Let's assume the bettor has placed both a pass bet and an any crap bet, and a crap has been rolled. The bettor feels smug. He has recovered the loss on his pass bet. The dice are now coming out again, so what does he do? He places the same size of bet on pass and the same size of bet as before on any craps. His "friendly dealer" has probably assisted him in doing this by handing him seven units from his any crap bet, leaving his one-unit bet on any craps with instructions that he "insure" his bet again.

There are those who will argue that every roll of the dice is a new roll and that it has no relationship to anything that has happened before. This is just plain baloney! When a crap has just been rolled and the bettor is betting that another crap will be rolled on the next roll, he is betting that two consecutive craps will be rolled. The fact that he is making this bet *after* the first crap roll of the dice instead of before the first crap is immaterial.

The probability against rolling the first crap was 9 to 1 (36 to 4). The probability against rolling two consecutive craps is 81 to 1 (9 x 9). The return ratio when one unit is permitted to double is (8 x 8) ÷ 81 x 100 = 79.01%. The return ratio when seven units are removed after the first crap with only one unit being left as the bet on the second roll is (7 + 8) ÷ 81 x 100 = 18.52%.

When you place a second consecutive crap bet, you're placing your money on a bet with a probability return ratio of 18.52% when you could have bet your money to pass at a probability return ratio of 98.59%. If two consecutive craps have been rolled and you place a third any crap bet of the same unit size as the first two, you're placing your money on a bet with a 3.02% probability return ratio.

Who can blame casino dealers for encouraging bettors to "buy insurance" at these prices? Bets like these give the casino high yields at low risk and help make them wealthy.

The following chart shows the actual consecutive crap rolls for the five casinos and a comparison of them to their probability distributions.

| CONSECUTIVE CRAP ROLLS | | | | | |
|---|---|---|---|---|---|
| | 1 | 2 | 3 | 4 | TOTAL CRAPS ROLLED |
| Frontier | 90 | 17 | 0 | 0 | 124 |
| Hilton | 92 | 11 | 1 | 0 | 117 |
| Caesars | 129 | 7 | 3 | 1 | 156 |
| Sands | 114 | 12 | 2 | 0 | 144 |
| Nugget | 228 | 25 | 2 | 0 | 284 |
| 40-Hour Total | 653 | 72 | 8 | 1 | 825 |
| Probability | 673 | 75 | 8 | 1 | 851 |

There were (72 ÷ 653) = 1/9 as many double consecutive craps than there were single ones, and (8 ÷653) = 1/81 as many triple consecutive craps as single ones. The data confirm the reasons previously given for not betting on any craps with such poor returns.

# 2, 12, 3, 11

Like the field and any crap bets, 2, 12, 3 and 11 are numbers on which a bet lasts for one roll only. Players very seldom place bets on 2, 12 and 3 because they are usually covered as "insurance" by a bet on any craps. But 11 gets a sizeable play, especially on the first roll. And what happens if an 11 is rolled? The bettor, assisted by the dealer, removes his winnings and leaves the same unit bet to face the next roll, which must complete the second part of a consecutive double in order to win.

The return on 11 is not good at best. For a single bet at a Las Vegas Strip casino where the casino pays 15 for 1, the return ratio is 83.33%. If the bet is permitted to parlay, the return ratio is 69.44%. If allowed to parlay again it is 57.87%. If the winnings are withdrawn each time and only one unit is left as a bet, the return ratio on the second is only 17.9%, and on the third it would be 1.99%.

> The casinos love players who bet on 11. The house makes money on it, no matter how you play it.

The following charts show the performances of the 2, 12, 11 and 3 at the five casinos. Out of the 7,654 rolls of the dice, only the 11 had any consecutive triples—a probability of once out of 6,802 rolls—and it had two. It was not surprising that neither the 2 nor 12 had any consecutive triples, as the probability for either of them is one out of 46,656 rolls.

| 2 CONSECUTIVE ROLLS | | | |
|---|---|---|---|
| | 1 | 2 | 3 | TOTAL |
| Frontier | 29 | 1 | 0 | 31 |
| Hilton | 30 | 2 | 0 | 34 |
| Caesars | 43 | 0 | 0 | 43 |
| Sands | 31 | 2 | 0 | 35 |
| Nugget | 59 | 4 | 0 | 67 |
| 40-Hour Total | 192 | 9 | 0 | 210 |
| Probability | 202 | 5½ | 0 | 213 |

| 12<br>CONSECUTIVE ROLLS | | | |
|---|---|---|---|
| | 1 | 2 | 3 | TOTAL |
| Frontier | 31 | 1 | 0 | 33 |
| Hilton | 26 | 2 | 0 | 30 |
| Caesars | 28 | 0 | 0 | 28 |
| Sands | 29 | 1 | 0 | 31 |
| Nugget | 58 | 1 | 0 | 60 |
| 40-Hour Total | 172 | 5 | 0 | 182 |
| Probability | 202 | 5½ | 0 | 213 |

| 3<br>CONSECUTIVE ROLLS | | | |
|---|---|---|---|
| | 1 | 2 | 3 | TOTAL |
| Frontier | 58 | 1 | 0 | 60 |
| Hilton | 45 | 4 | 0 | 53 |
| Caesars | 81 | 2 | 0 | 85 |
| Sands | 72 | 3 | 0 | 78 |
| Nugget | 143 | 7 | 0 | 157 |
| 40-Hour Total | 399 | 17 | 0 | 433 |
| Probability | 380 | 21 | 1 | 425 |

| 11<br>CONSECUTIVE ROLLS | | | |
|---|---|---|---|
| | 1 | 2 | 3 | TOTAL |
| Frontier | 44 | 1 | 0 | 46 |
| Hilton | 56 | 3 | 0 | 62 |
| Caesars | 63 | 5 | 1 | 76 |
| Sands | 64 | 2 | 1 | 71 |
| Nugget | 138 | 3 | 0 | 144 |
| 40-Hour Total | 365 | 14 | 2 | 399 |
| Probability | 380 | 21 | 1 | 425 |

The 2, 12, 3 and 11 performed closely to their probabilities, thus there were no surprises or opportunities for any productive winnings with any of these bets.

# HARDWAY BETS

Hardway bets differ from bets such as field, craps, 2, 3, 12 and 11 in that they are not bets that must be decided by the next one roll of the dice. A hardway bet presupposes that the particular hardway number will be rolled before either a 7 or the same dice total made up of other dice numbers is rolled. Consequently, a consecutive hardway category means two or more of the same hardway number have been rolled before either a 7 or a different dice makeup of this number is rolled.

It does not mean that the same hardway number has been rolled back to back. There could be many dice numbers other than 7 or the same dice total rolled between the consecutive hardways.

Like the crap and 11 bets, when a hardway number is rolled, the bettor (again aided by the dealer) often removes his winnings and leaves his unit bet, thus changing his bet to a unit bet that faces a consecutive probability return ratio as low as 15% for double consecutive and 2% for triple consecutive!

The following charts show the actual hardway consecutive data from the five casinos and comparisons to the probabilities.

### HARDWAY 4 CONSECUTIVE ROLLS

|  | 1 | 2 | 3 | 4 | 5 | TOTAL |
|---|---|---|---|---|---|---|
| Frontier | 26 | 5 | 0 | 0 | 0 | 36 |
| Hilton | 28 | 1 | 1 | 0 | 0 | 33 |
| Caesars | 29 | 8 | 1 | 0 | 0 | 48 |
| Sands | 27 | 3 | 2 | 0 | 0 | 39 |
| Nugget | 52 | 7 | 1 | 0 | 0 | 69 |
| 40-Hour Total | 162 | 24 | 5 | 0 | 0 | 225 |
| Probability | 168 | 19 | 2 | ¼ | 0 | 213 |

### HARDWAY 10 CONSECUTIVE ROLLS

|  | 1 | 2 | 3 | 4 | 5 | TOTAL |
|---|---|---|---|---|---|---|
| Frontier | 31 | 1 | 0 | 0 | 0 | 33 |
| Hilton | 13 | 1 | 0 | 0 | 0 | 15 |
| Caesars | 38 | 3 | 0 | 0 | 0 | 44 |
| Sands | 33 | 4 | 1 | 0 | 0 | 44 |
| Nugget | 55 | 5 | 0 | 0 | 0 | 65 |
| 40-Hour Total | 170 | 14 | 1 | 0 | 0 | 201 |
| Probability | 168 | 19 | 2 | ¼ | 0 | 213 |

### HARDWAY 6 CONSECUTIVE ROLLS

|  | 1 | 2 | 3 | 4 | 5 | TOTAL |
|---|---|---|---|---|---|---|
| Frontier | 27 | 2 | 0 | 0 | 0 | 31 |
| Hilton | 17 | 0 | 1 | 0 | 1 | 25 |
| Caesars | 31 | 2 | 0 | 0 | 0 | 35 |
| Sands | 32 | 3 | 0 | 0 | 0 | 38 |
| Nugget | 63 | 5 | 0 | 0 | 0 | 73 |
| 40-Hour Total | 170 | 12 | 1 | 0 | 1 | 202 |
| Probability | 176 | 16 | 1 ½ | 1/8 | 0 | 213 |

| HARDWAY 8 CONSECUTIVE ROLLS | | | | | | |
|---|---|---|---|---|---|---|
| | 1 | 2 | 3 | 4 | 5 | TOTAL |
| Frontier | 22 | 1 | 0 | 0 | 0 | 24 |
| Hilton | 19 | 2 | 0 | 0 | 0 | 23 |
| Caesars | 37 | 3 | 2 | 0 | 0 | 49 |
| Sands | 40 | 4 | 0 | 0 | 0 | 48 |
| Nugget | 47 | 7 | 3 | 0 | 0 | 70 |
| 40-Hour Total | 165 | 17 | 5 | 0 | 0 | 214 |
| Probability | 176 | 16 | 1 ½ | 1/8 | 0 | 213 |

# 7

The game of craps is constructed around the dice number 7. If a 7 is thrown on the coming out roll, it wins. At all other times when a 7 appears, all working bets on the table lose, except for the established don't pass and don't come, as well as any come bet that was coming out on that roll. The table is thus cleared of all betting chips before the next hand is started with a new shooter.

In order for you to have a fair chance to benefit from any of the side bets (sucker bets), there must be sufficient rolls between 7's for these bets to satisfy the requirements of their probabilities. For example, if you place a side bet on 6, you should hope for more than seven rolls before a 7 is rolled because the probability for a 6 will appear five times for every 36 rolls, which figures to be once every 7.2 rolls of the dice.

The following charts show results from the five casinos for 7's and non-7's (consecutive rolls of the dice between rolls of 7).

| 7 CONSECUTIVE ROLLS | | | | | | |
|---|---|---|---|---|---|---|
|  | 1 | 2 | 3 | 4 | 5 | TOTAL |
| **Frontier** | 125 | 15 | 2 | 0 | 1 | **166** |
| **Hilton** | 106 | 9 | 1 | 0 | 0 | **127** |
| **Caesars** | 182 | 30 | 10 | 3 | 0 | **284** |
| **Sands** | 176 | 29 | 6 | 0 | 1 | **257** |
| **Nugget** | 299 | 48 | 8 | 3 | 0 | **431** |
| **40-Hour Total** | **888** | **131** | **27** | **6** | **2** | **1,265** |
| **Probability** | **882** | **149** | **25** | **4** | **1** | **1,276** |

# EXPOSING THE FALLACIES

## NON-7'S CONSECUTIVE NON-7 ROLLS

| | 1 | 2 | 3 | 4 | 5 | 6 | 7 | 8 | 9 | 10 | 11 | 12 | 13 | 14 | 15 | 16 | 17 | 18 | 19 | 20 |
|---|---|---|---|---|---|---|---|---|---|---|---|---|---|---|---|---|---|---|---|---|
| Frontier | 17 | 22 | 20 | 12 | 8 | 13 | 9 | 8 | 4 | 3 | 3 | 6 | 2 | 3 | 2 | 2 | 2 | 2 | 0 | 1 |
| Hilton | 10 | 21 | 19 | 10 | 7 | 5 | 6 | 10 | 3 | 2 | 3 | 3 | 1 | 2 | 2 | 1 | 2 | 1 | 0 | 0 |
| Caesars | 45 | 40 | 21 | 25 | 22 | 6 | 10 | 9 | 6 | 6 | 6 | 2 | 6 | 3 | 6 | 1 | 0 | 0 | 5 | 0 |
| Sands | 35 | 31 | 30 | 17 | 22 | 13 | 8 | 6 | 11 | 8 | 11 | 4 | 1 | 2 | 2 | 2 | 2 | 1 | 1 | 1 |
| Nugget | 59 | 53 | 45 | 29 | 29 | 21 | 16 | 16 | 19 | 8 | 11 | 9 | 3 | 8 | 4 | 2 | 5 | 5 | 3 | 1 |
| 40-Hour Total | 166 | 167 | 135 | 93 | 88 | 58 | 49 | 49 | 43 | 27 | 34 | 24 | 13 | 18 | 16 | 8 | 11 | 9 | 9 | 3 |
| Probability | 177 | 148 | 123 | 103 | 85 | 71 | 59 | 50 | 42 | 35 | 29 | 24 | 20 | 16½ | 14 | 11½ | 9½ | 8 | 6½ | 5½ |

| | 21 | 22 | 23 | 24 | 25 | 26 | 27 | 28 | 29 | 30 | 31 | 32 | 33 | 34 | 35 | 36 | 37 | 38 | 39 | 40 |
|---|---|---|---|---|---|---|---|---|---|---|---|---|---|---|---|---|---|---|---|---|
| Frontier | 0 | 0 | 1 | 2 | 0 | 0 | 0 | 0 | 0 | 0 | 0 | 0 | 0 | 0 | 0 | 0 | 1 | 0 | 0 | 0 |
| Hilton | 2 | 2 | 1 | 0 | 0 | 0 | 0 | 0 | 0 | 0 | 1 | 0 | 0 | 0 | 1 | 0 | 1 | 0 | 0 | 1 |
| Caesars | 0 | 1 | 0 | 3 | 0 | 0 | 0 | 0 | 1 | 0 | 0 | 0 | 0 | 0 | 0 | 0 | 0 | 0 | 0 | 1 |
| Sands | 0 | 0 | 1 | 1 | 0 | 0 | 0 | 1 | 0 | 0 | 0 | 0 | 0 | 0 | 0 | 0 | 0 | 0 | 0 | 1 |
| Nugget | 4 | 1 | 0 | 1 | 1 | 0 | 1 | 1 | 0 | 1 | 1 | 1 | 0 | 0 | 0 | 0 | 0 | 0 | 0 | 0 |
| 40-Hour Total | 6 | 4 | 3 | 7 | 1 | 0 | 1 | 2 | 1 | 1 | 2 | 1 | 0 | 0 | 1 | 0 | 2 | 0 | 0 | 2 |
| Probability | 4½ | 3½ | 3 | 2¾ | 2¼ | 2 | 1½ | 1¼ | 1 | 7/8 | 3/4 | 5/8 | 1/2 | 7/16 | 3/8 | 5/16 | ¼ | ¼ | ¼ | ¼ |

The large number of consecutive non-7 rolls do not necessarily occur as rolls thrown during one pass bet decision—unless that decision happens to be a losing one ending with a 7 or a winning one whose following decision has a coming out 7. The large numbers of consecutive non-7 rolls usually span several pass decisions, thus encouraging the place bettor to keep his place bets on the table.

All bets except for come bets and don't come bets can be off during a new coming out roll. The dealers encourage this because if the coming out roll is not a 7, it could be a winner for the sucker bettor, especially during a long non-7 series.

## HOW LONG IS A PASS BET DECISION?

Because a sucker bettor is concerned with how many non-7 rolls the shooter might throw, we should examine how many rolls of the dice can be expected for each pass, pass loss, and don't pass decision.

Our calculations show that the probable number of rolls for each pass bet decision (win or lose) is 3.36. The probable number of rolls for each pass decision is 2.98. The probable number of rolls for each pass-loss decision is 3.74. And the probable number of rolls for each don't pass win decision is 3.90.

| PROBABLE # OF ROLLS | |
|---|---|
| TYPE OF DECISION | PROBABLE # ROLLS |
| Pass Bet Decision | 2.98 |
| Pass Loss Decision | 3.74 |
| Pass Win Decision | 3.90 |

The following chart of the data from the five casinos shows how their performances compared with their probabilities.

| | NO. OF PASS BET DECISIONS | NUMBER OF PASSES | NUMBER OF LOSSES | NUMBER OF DON'T PASS | TOTAL ROLLS OF DICE | DICE ROLLS FOR PASS | DICE ROLLS FOR LOSS | DICE ROLLS DON'T PASS | ROLLS PER PASS BET DECISIONS | ROLLS PER PASS | ROLLS PER LOSS | ROLLS PER DON'T PASS |
|---|---|---|---|---|---|---|---|---|---|---|---|---|
| **Frontier** | 299 | 139 | 160 | 154 | 1079 | 440 | 639 | 633 | 3.60 | 3.17 | 3.99 | 4.11 |
| **Hilton** | 234 | 110 | 124 | 119 | 930 | 379 | 551 | 546 | 3.55 | 3.45 | 4.44 | 4.59 |
| **Caesars** | 497 | 250 | 247 | 238 | 1548 | 710 | 838 | 829 | 3.12 | 2.84 | 3.39 | 3.48 |
| **Sands** | 450 | 222 | 228 | 221 | 1461 | 628 | 833 | 826 | 3.22 | 2.82 | 3.65 | 3.74 |
| **Nugget** | 740 | 353 | 387 | 372 | 2636 | 1131 | 1505 | 1490 | 3.56 | 3.20 | 3.89 | 4.01 |
| **40-Hour Total** | 2220 | 1074 | 1146 | 1104 | 7654 | 3288 | 4366 | 4324 | 3.45 | 3.06 | 3.81 | 3.92 |
| **Probability** | | | | | | | | | 3.36 | 2.98 | 3.74 | 3.90 |

We could take a casual look at these results, and see them as being merely academically interesting, both as to their values and as to the closeness of their probabilities to their actual performances. However, these ratios become far more interesting when we relate them to the advice we so often receive from "friendly expert" crap table dealers.

Dealers will take place bets, hardway bets, and come bet odds off on each new coming out roll. They do this as a service because a 7 would make losses out of all these bets if they were not off.

> Expect a 7 on the coming out roll once in every six times.

It is a fact that a 7 would make losers out of these bets, no doubt about it. But how often should we expect a 7 to appear on the coming out roll? Once in six times is the answer.

Also, once in six times, either an 11 or a crap should appear on the coming out roll, but these would not turn the place bets, hardway bets, or come bet odds into losers. They would not affect them in any way. Assuming that each place bet has been covered, the odds are 4 to 2 that the roll will produce a winner,

and it is only 1 to 5 that it will produce a loser. By convincing you that you should have these bets off on the coming out roll, the casino crap dealer has lowered the probability return for all these bets.

Let's see by how much.

The probability ratio for rolls-per-pass is 2.98. This means that on the 2.98th dice roll, the pass point will be rolled and a new point will be started, which will also consist of 2.98 dice rolls if it becomes a pass. Now, if place bets, hardway bets, or come bet odds were to be off on the new coming out roll, the number of possible rolls in which any of these could be completed would be reduced from 2.98 to 1.98. This would make the probability return on these bets become 66.44% (1.98 ÷ 2.74 x 100 = 66.44%) of whatever percent they had been. This would increase the probability of loss on these bets by a factor of 33.56%

On the other hand, if the new point turned out to be a loss whose number of rolls is 3.74, there would have been only 2.74 possible winning rolls to begin with, including the coming out roll, because the last roll would have to be a losing 7. If the coming out roll had been off, this would make the possible return on the bets become 33.5% (1.74 ÷ 2.74 x 100 = 63.51% of whatever percent they had been. The losses in this case would be increased by a factor of 36.5%.

In order to arrive at a single loss percent, we will consider the basic loss-win distribution of 1,004 to 976 and compute the loss percent as being 33.05% (1,004 x 36.5 + 976 x 33.56 ÷ 1980 = 35.05%).

This loss percent has been computed on the theory that each coming out roll would be a winner. This is not true because out of 36 coming out rolls, six should be 7's, four should be craps, and two should be 11's, thus reducing the number of winning coming out rolls to 24. Consequently, the loss percent would be 23.37% (35.05 x (24 ÷ 36) = 23.37%).

To put this another way, if the usual practice of having bets off on the coming out rolls were changed to having them working on the coming out rolls, profits would be increased by 30.5%.

$$(100.00 \div 76.63) - 1.00 \times 100 = 30.5\%.$$

# WHAT IS THE DISTRIBUTION OF ROLLS IN A DECISION?

While standing at a crap table, you have probably observed that sometimes a roller completes a pass bet decision with one roll of the dice by rolling a 7, 11, or a crap; and that sometimes he takes a great number of rolls before either winning or losing. The total number of pass bet decisions encountered in the five casinos was 2,220 of which 1,074 were passes, 1,146 were losses, and 1,104 were don't pass wins. These were distributed among many different passes and losses of different numbers of rolls. The charts on the following page show how their distributions compared to their probabilities.

Because some pass bet decisions contain quite a few rolls—and because when these occur, it appears that the sucker bettors are making big money—it is quite easy for an "observer" (a player who has not yet graduated into experimenting with the exotic sucker bets) to become misled about what the chances for success with these bets are.

As we can see from the tabulations, during the course of an evening, it is normal for many decisions to consist of twelve or more dice rolls. The occurrences of these long-roll decisions are few and far between—but each one leaves a sucker bettor hoping that another such long-roll decision will happen soon and bail him out from his losses. These long-roll decisions also encourage the uninitiated to try a few of these newly-discovered bets.

The casino does not lose because of any of these long-roll decisions. It might lose temporarily because of heavy betting during one streak, but it will recoup these losses in a very short time. How? Because the sucker bettors will try to influence the happening of another long-roll decision by betting heavily that it will happen during the next few hands.

## PASS
### NUMBER OF ROLLS PER PASS

| | 1 | 2 | 3 | 4 | 5 | 6 | 7 | 8 | 9 | 10 | 11 | 12 | 13 | 14 | 15 | 16 | 17 | 18 | 19 | 20 | 21 | 22 | 23 | 24 |
|---|---|---|---|---|---|---|---|---|---|---|---|---|---|---|---|---|---|---|---|---|---|---|---|---|
| Frontier | 54 | 28 | 11 | 14 | 7 | 8 | 5 | 2 | 6 | 1 | 1 | 0 | 1 | 0 | 0 | 0 | 0 | 0 | 1 | | | | | |
| Hilton | 36 | 29 | 10 | 7 | 6 | 9 | 1 | 4 | 0 | 1 | 2 | 2 | 2 | 0 | 0 | 0 | 0 | 0 | 0 | 0 | 0 | 1 | | |
| Caesars | 123 | 35 | 27 | 18 | 10 | 9 | 6 | 6 | 2 | 4 | 4 | 2 | 0 | 0 | 0 | 0 | 0 | 0 | 1 | 0 | 0 | 0 | 0 | 1 |
| Sands | 93 | 41 | 28 | 16 | 12 | 14 | 3 | 8 | 3 | 1 | 0 | 2 | 0 | 0 | 1 | | | | | | | | | |
| Nugget | 164 | 46 | 28 | 24 | 28 | 14 | 19 | 5 | 6 | 2 | 5 | 5 | 2 | 1 | 1 | 0 | 1 | 1 | 1 | | | | | |
| 40-Hour Total | 470 | 179 | 104 | 79 | 63 | 54 | 34 | 25 | 17 | 9 | 12 | 11 | 5 | 1 | 2 | 0 | 1 | 1 | 3 | 0 | 0 | 1 | 0 | 1 |
| Probability | 493 | 171 | 125 | 90 | 64 | 46 | 33 | 24 | 17 | 12 | 9 | 6 | 4 | 3 | 2½ | 1¾ | 1¼ | 1 | ½ | ¼ | | | | |

## DON'T PASS
### NUMBER OF ROLLS PER DON'T PASS

| | 1 | 2 | 3 | 4 | 5 | 6 | 7 | 8 | 9 | 10 | 11 | 12 | 13 | 14 | 15 | 16 | 17 | 18 | 19 | 20 | 21 | 22 | 23 | 24 |
|---|---|---|---|---|---|---|---|---|---|---|---|---|---|---|---|---|---|---|---|---|---|---|---|---|
| Frontier | 28 | 30 | 22 | 22 | 13 | 8 | 10 | 6 | 7 | 3 | 1 | 0 | 3 | 0 | 0 | 0 | 1 | | | | | | | |
| Hilton | 17 | 20 | 22 | 17 | 9 | 10 | 2 | 6 | 8 | 0 | 2 | 2 | 0 | 1 | 1 | 0 | 0 | 1 | 0 | 0 | 0 | 0 | 1 | |
| Caesars | 50 | 64 | 42 | 20 | 18 | 17 | 9 | 4 | 9 | 0 | 2 | 2 | 1 | 0 | 0 | 0 | 0 | 0 | 0 | 1 | | | | |
| Sands | 40 | 50 | 39 | 30 | 19 | 13 | 12 | 7 | 4 | 0 | 2 | 0 | 0 | 2 | 1 | 0 | 1 | | | | | | | |
| Nugget | 61 | 78 | 69 | 44 | 29 | 31 | 13 | 14 | 9 | 10 | 5 | 3 | 3 | 0 | 3 | | | | | | | | | |
| 40-Hour Total | 196 | 242 | 194 | 133 | 88 | 79 | 46 | 37 | 37 | 13 | 12 | 7 | 7 | 3 | 5 | 0 | 2 | 2 | 0 | 1 | 0 | 0 | 1 | |
| Probability | 185 | 247 | 180 | 130 | 93 | 67 | 48 | 35 | 25 | 18 | 13 | 9 | 7 | 5 | 4 | 3 | 2 | 2½ | 1 | ¾ | ½ | ¼ | 1 | |

# HOW LARGE IS A HAND?

A **hand** is completed when the roller throws a 7 after having established a point on a coming out roll. With this 7, the shooter loses his point and he loses the dice to the player on his left.

Before losing this decision and the dice, he may have completed several other decisions, some of which may have been coming out naturals (7's or 11's) for winners or coming out craps for losers. Some of them may have been point decisions whose coming out numbers were matched by dice numbers on later rolls.

Regardless of what combinations of whatever types of decisions make up a hand, the hand ends when a 7 is rolled on any roll other than a coming out one. Consequently, it becomes obvious that the number of hands must be exactly equal to the total number of 7's rolled on all rolls after the coming out rolls. For the five casinos, that number was 909.

The probability for the number of decisions in a hand (both win and lose) is 2.52. For the five casinos, there were 2,220 pass bet decisions distributed among 908 hands for an average of 2.44 decisions per hand.

Since some hands consist of *one* decision and some consist of *two* decisions, there must be many hands with more than 2.52 decisions. The following tabulations show a comparison of the actual results at the five casinos to the probability.

| DECISIONS PER HAND | | | | | | | | | | | | | | | | |
|---|---|---|---|---|---|---|---|---|---|---|---|---|---|---|---|---|
| | 1 | 2 | 3 | 4 | 5 | 6 | 7 | 8 | 9 | 10 | 11 | 12 | 13 | 14 | 15 | # OF HANDS | NO 7'S AFTER 1ST ROLL |
| Frontier | 59 | 25 | 15 | 11 | 7 | 4 | 2 | 2 | 0 | 0 | 0 | 1 | 0 | 0 | 0 | 126 | 126 |
| Hilton | 42 | 28 | 13 | 10 | 5 | 1 | 1 | 0 | 1 | 1 | 0 | 0 | 0 | 0 | 0 | 102 | 102 |
| Caesars | 68 | 47 | 28 | 16 | 14 | 5 | 3 | 4 | 1 | 0 | 1 | 0 | 1 | 0 | 0 | 189 | 189 |
| Sands | 76 | 40 | 25 | 13 | 12 | 5 | 5 | 3 | 2 | 0 | 0 | 0 | 0 | 0 | 0 | 181 | 181 |
| Nugget | 131 | 79 | 34 | 26 | 23 | 10 | 3 | 0 | 2 | 2 | 1 | 0 | 0 | 0 | 0 | 311 | 311 |
| 40-Hour Total | 376 | 219 | 115 | 76 | 61 | 25 | 14 | 9 | 6 | 3 | 2 | 1 | 1 | 0 | 0 | 909 | 909 |
| Probability | 365 | 217 | 129 | 77 | 46 | 27 | 16 | 10 | 6 | 3 | 2 | 1 | 1 | ½ | 1/5 | | |

Once again the actual results adhere closely to what probability dictates they should.

Now that we've examined all these computations and data, let's move forward to the next chapter, where we'll find out what exactly what they mean to us as crapshooters.

# 10 USING THE COMPUTATIONS AND DATA FOR AN EDGE

Now that we've examined the math, looked at numerous computations, and investigated the resulting data, only one question remains: What does it all mean for us lovers of the game of craps?

## DICE PERFORMANCE VERSUS THEORETICAL PROBABILITY

One thing the data show us is that dice perform very closely to their theoretical probabilities. Data suggest that each surge of concentrated action is followed very soon by short, pass bet decisions and short hands, thus showing that the dice react quickly in order to maintain their probability balances.

These rapid shifts from concentrated action periods to short ones do *not* suggest that you should change from pass to don't pass at these times. This means no such thing! Always remember that there will be twice as many single-point pass decisions as single-point loss decisions (eight naturals to four craps). Further, there will be eight to three times as many single-roll passes as there are single-roll don't passes.

What the data suggests is that whenever there has been a surge of concentrated action, you should refrain from playing

any of the side bets, because they have become full-fledged sucker bets.

We have all stood at a crap table and witnessed some bettor throw three or four 7's in a row or have a long hand with long decisions and said to ourselves, "If he can do it, so can I!" And then, after he has finally rolled a losing 7 and the dice have passed to us, we have approached our betting as though this same thing were going to happen right now. As a result, we quickly lost everything on our own hand that we had won on that previous hot hand.

Failures like that one did not occur because the other fellow could roll the dice better than we could. They occurred because we were at the wrong place at the wrong time with the wrong bet.

Instead of saying, "If he can do it," we should have said, "If it can happen to him." We should have said *happen* instead of *do*. Why? Because the roller was simply the vehicle that propelled the dice onto the table at that time. Not one physical action of his exerted any intentional positive control over the result of any one of his rolls! He just happened to be in the right place at the right time when the dice turned hot.

> Let me make this clear: No intentional physical action exerts any positive control over the dice, no matter what other books or hucksters lead you to believe.

The complete idea that we should have envisioned was, "If it can happen to him, it can also happen to me at some time— but the probability is that it will not happen on the hand that directly follows his."

Even after looking at the computations of the probabilities in this book, and after viewing the closeness with which the actual data performed to these probabilities, many people will continue to argue that each roll of the dice is a new start; and therefore, theory and probability have nothing to do with what will occur on a crap table during any period or at any time.

It is true that each roll of the dice is the beginning of something new. Each first roll when I began recording my data at each of the five casinos was the beginning of a series of rolls that I was about to record. But just because each was the beginning of something new—a new series—it did not mean that each series would be so different than those before it that probability might not hold for this new series. Instead, whether for five or 10 hours, each series performed closely to what the probabilities dictated that it should. We can also say that the first roll of the dice at the Frontier was the beginning of a 40-hour series of dice rolls, even though time intervals occurred between the recording of the individual series at the other casinos.

We can expand this theme by saying that this same thing is true for an individual. Each individual represents just one series of dice rolls in his entire lifetime. Each person's series started with the first roll of dice that he witnessed and consists, in their order of rolling, each roll of the dice he has witnessed since then, regardless of the time intervals between any of them—because if he had recorded each one of these rolls and if he now tabulates the results, he would have a tabulation of all the probabilities in the game of craps.

We can further state that if an individual constantly approaches every coming out roll and every hand and every sucker bet with the same attitude and betting procedure as each time before, his performance at the crap table will be a consistent loss equal to the amount he has bet multiplied by the casino's percent of the probability percents of his betting selections.

Our argumentative disbeliever might agree to the logic of our arguments, but he will still argue that theory is one thing and that an actual happening is another thing—and he will quote many examples that he allegedly has witnessed.

## MAKING SUCKER BETS

Now, let's look at some betting opportunities that occurred during our 40 hours at the five casinos.

If a bettor cannot resist the temptation to dabble in place bets, he should observe the rule concerning parlaying sucker bets. We have seen computations showing that the bettor should let his sucker bets parlay by the amount of each win, or he should withdraw both the win and the bet.

If the bettor withdraws only the win and leaves the same bet on the place number, he greatly lowers the percent of the return his bet could yield. To illustrate this we will look at three actual situations that occurred at three of the casinos.

1. The Hilton had a hand that, before a 7 was rolled, had three 4's, seven 5's, four 6's, two 8's, seven 9's, and eight 10's.
2. Caesars had a hand that, before a 7 was rolled, had four 4's, three 5's, eight 6's, five 8's, five 9's, and eight 10's.
3. The Sands had a hand that, before a 7 was rolled, had five 4's, seven 5's, five 6's, five 8's, five 9's, and eight 10's.

To compute the maximum possible return from these, we will assume that $5 place bets ($6 on 6 and 8 were placed on all the place bet numbers on the coming out roll of the first pass bet decision, and they were working on all of the coming out rolls which followed. We will also assume that all winnings were immediately added to the bet on the place bet number that had just won until such time as a casino maximum bet of

$5,000 appeared on a number. We will make a final assumption that all the place bets were removed after the roll that came just before the losing 7 was rolled.

In this way we will determine what the maximum return could have been for each situation, having started each one with the minimum bet permitted for betting on all the place bet numbers, which is $32.

| MAXIMUM RETURNS | | | |
|---|---|---|---|
| | BET | RETURNED | PROFIT |
| **Hilton** | $32 | $20,203 | $20,171 |
| **Caesars** | $32 | $20,066 | $20,024 |
| **Sands** | $32 | $13,198 | $13,166 |
| **Totals** | $96 | $53,457 | $53,361 |

Next, we follow the advice of our "friendly expert" dealer by having the place bets off during all coming out rolls and by also having removed all winnings each time a place bet number has been rolled.

| RETURNS USING DEALER ADVICE | | | |
|---|---|---|---|
| | BET | RETURNED | PROFIT |
| **Hilton** | $32 | $211 | $179 |
| **Caesars** | $32 | $246 | $214 |
| **Sands** | $32 | $239 | $207 |
| **Totals** | $96 | $696 | $600 |

Now let's construct a third case where the betting is the same as in the last one. Recall that we followed the advice of our "friendly expert" dealer by being off during all coming out rolls and we removed the winnings each time the dealer handed them to us after each place bet number had been rolled.

In this case, however, our bets will be $500 on each place bet number ($600 on 6 and 8) for a total betting amount of $3,200.

| RETURNS USING DEALER ADVICE | | | |
|---|---|---|---|
| | BET | RETURNED | PROFIT |
| Hilton | $3,200 | $21,100 | $17,900 |
| Caesars | $3,200 | $24,600 | $21,400 |
| Sands | $3,200 | $23,900 | $20,700 |
| Totals | $9,600 | $69,600 | $60,000 |

These winnings compare closely to the ones in the first scenario where the total bet in each case was $32 and the place bets were permitted to parlay. Now ask the question, "Why risk $3,200 when $32 might do the job?" The casinos love people who bet this $3,200 way!

Everyone's bankroll has more $32 bets than it has $3,200 bets. As a matter of fact, there are 100 times as many $32 bets as $3,200 bets. This means that the place bets with parlaying could be attempted 100 times with $32 for each one time that a non-parlay attempt could be made with $3,200.

Let's see what the effects would have been if we had kept the place bets in the $3,200 scenario working on the coming out rolls, while continuing to pick up the winnings after each place bet number had been rolled.

| RETURNS KEEP PLACE BETS /PICK UP WINNINGS | | | |
|---|---|---|---|
| | BET | RETURNED | PROFIT |
| Hilton | $3,200 | $27,100 | $23,900 |
| Caesars | $3,200 | $28,700 | $25,500 |
| Sands | $3,200 | $30,100 | $26,900 |
| Totals | $9,600 | $85,900 | $76,300 |

These results show an increase of 27.17% in profit by having the place bets working on the coming out rolls ($76,300 when working and $60,000 profit when not working). This should ring a bell! Thinking back, recall that we computed a winning increase of 30.5% for having the place bets working on the coming out rolls.

Strange, isn't it, how the probabilities of the game are continuously confirmed by the actual performance of the dice?

Now let's examine another mind boggler. At the Hilton, there was one time when five consecutive hardway 6's appeared—not back-to-back 6's—but five hardway 6's, between which there were no 7's or easy-way 6's. If there had been no betting limit, and if these five hardway 6's been parlayed, a $1 bet would have become worth $100,000 for a $99,999 win!

On the other hand, if five single bets had been made instead, it would have taken five bets of $2,222.20—a total risk of $11,111—to accomplish what $1 could have done!

## PARLAYING SUCKER BETS

These examples illustrate the reason why, when you're betting any of the side bets (sucker bets) *where odds are given*, you should let your bets parlay. Further, you should have them working on the coming out rolls until you're satisfied with your profit—at which time you should pick up your entire bet. Either do it this way, or don't bet at all.

The dice offer opportunities where our fantasies could occur and where our crap dreams could be realized. The problem is how to be there at the right time, with the right bet, and with the courage to see it through. The unanswered question is, "How do we recognize these opportunities before they occur and not recognize them only after they have happened?"

We can only say that the answer is the key to opening the gate to Fantasyland's Garden of Eden. Like the Fountain of Youth, people will always be searching for it.

Now let's travel forward in the next chapter to a winning approach.

# 11 THE WINNING APPROACH

During our travels through the chapters of this book, we completed the distance of 7,654 rolls of the dice down five casino crap tables in 40 hours at a cost of 72 betting units. This expense was based on our traveling the Pass Route instead of the Don't Pass Trail, where we would have collected a profit of 31 betting units. While progressing in our journey, we observed that the dice followed the paths that probability said they should follow. And we learned that whenever the dice veered from these paths, they quickly corrected and got back on course.

Our travels led us past sucker bets and through Fantasyland where consecutive happenings could lead to large winnings. There we learned that consecutive events do happen—but we found no way to predict exactly *when* they would happen. We also learned that a consecutive event in one direction would be counterbalanced at some time by either an opposite consecutive event of the same size or by a series of smaller opposite ones.

We also learned that although trap and sucker bets were more exciting than pass and don't pass, their probability returns were less than for pass and don't pass.

Our final realization was that if we follow either pass or don't pass long enough, we pay a tax of $1.41 for each $100 speculated. We found out that we probably would not lose the family fortune through this 1.41% tax, but we wouldn't increase it either.

# HOW CAN WE MAKE A PROFIT AT DICE?

We now arrive at our main problem at the craps table. What should we do in order to produce profits instead of losses? The answer is as simple as the question: In order to make a profit, we should bet pass when the dice will pass, and we should bet don't pass when the dice will lose. It is just that simple—except for one thing: How do we determine when the dice will either pass or don't pass on the next betting decision?

The answer isn't quite as simple as the question. We do not have any way of *exactly* determining what the dice will do on any next betting decision, or on any next roll, or on any next anything. So now we're back to where we were in the beginning. We're back to guessing—or are we? Have we uncovered something of value in the chapters of this book? Let's explore the answer to that question, beginning with betting when you're losing.

# TWO RULES OF BETTING WHEN YOU'RE LOSING

Probably the same as everyone else addicted to craps, I have observed dice appear to run in cycles. Many times when I began playing at a table, I experienced a period of winning, always followed by what appeared to be a long period of losing before any effective consecutive winning hands appeared. During the depths of these losing periods, I reversed the direction of my betting from pass to don't pass—only to have the dice reverse to pass wins. There also have been many times when I've attempted to recover my losses by placing large bets, usually with sad results.

In both of these two types of attempts at recovering losses, I violated two very important rules. First, I never should have changed the direction of my betting unless I intended to follow the new direction to a conclusion. Second, I never should have attempted to recover my losses with a single, large bet. These are two no-no's of craps! No one can consistently outguess the dice for any next roll or for any next individual betting decision.

---

### TWO NO-NO'S IN CRAPS

- Never change the direction of your betting unless you intend to follow the new direction to a conclusion.
- Never attempt to recover losses with a single, large bet.

---

# FLUCTUATIONS IN WINS AND LOSSES

One of the purposes behind my collecting data was to study whether dice fluctuated in cycles and, if they did, to study the lengths of these cycles. On page 137 are plotted curves showing the win and loss fluctuations for each of the five casinos. The horizontal curve shows the pass bet decisions that were completed at each casino table. The vertical shows the cumulative winnings or losses created by the winning or losing of each successive decision with a single unit of betting.

The horizontal lengths (total pass bet decisions) vary considerably between the casinos. The Frontier and Hilton hotels each represent five hours of data, whereas Caesars, the

Sands, and the Nugget each represent 10 hours. We might be led to believe that differences in the number of decisions in the horizontals would be governed by the number of rolls required for completing each decision; and that the fewer the decisions, the higher the number of rolls required for each one. But when we look back at the data, we see that this theory wouldn't hold. Why? Because the Frontier had the highest number of rolls per decision with 3.60, and the Nugget had the second highest ratio, 3.56.

The number of pass bet decisions that will be completed during any given time depends entirely upon how fast the dealers can pay off bets, clear the table of chips after decisions are completed, and get the dice rolling again. Consequently, the more crowded a table is, the longer it will take for the same number of dealers to pay off pass wins or clear the table of chips after pass losses.

Also, if a table has bettors playing the sucker bets, the dealers must take the time between each roll of the dice for paying and adjusting the betting chips into agreement with what the decisions have dictated. For example, when I was playing at the Nugget, there were very few periods when the table was even moderately crowded, probably due to its long time of downward motion. There also were very few players making sucker bets. As a result, the dice at the Nugget kept moving.

When a hot hand comes around and the players at the table begin cheering with each roll and continue to make sucker bets with each roll, the table normally becomes crowded, and an audience of onlookers usually migrates to the action. If we were to look at the amount of time that these hot hands lasted, we would be surprised at how long in minutes—*not* in rolls of the dice—they lasted. The reasons are obvious: The dealers have large numbers of bets to settle after each roll of the dice as well as after the conclusion of each decision. These long times between each roll and each decision make the shooter look more spectacular than he actually is because he holds the dice for such a long period of time.

## The Graphs

Curves for three different betting schemes were plotted for each hotel. The three curves for a hotel are plotted on one set of axes for easier comparison.

| LEGEND |
|---|
| ●●●●● Single Unit Bets |
| ▲▲▲▲▲ Single Unit Bets Plus Pass Odds Bets |
| ■■■■■ Single Unit Bets and Two-Unit Bets with Two-Unit Odds Bets on only the second pass bet decision of a hand, and only when the first pass bet decision had been a pass win |

**Frontier**

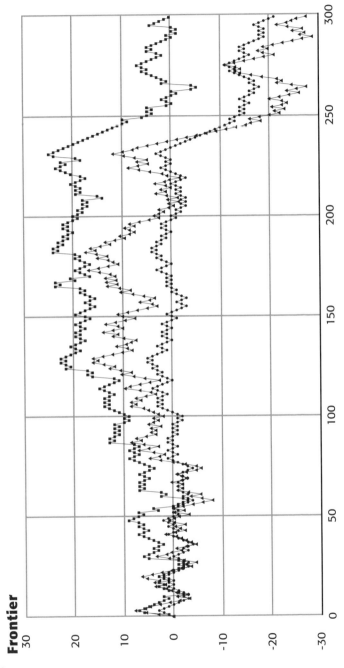

# THE WINNING APPROACH

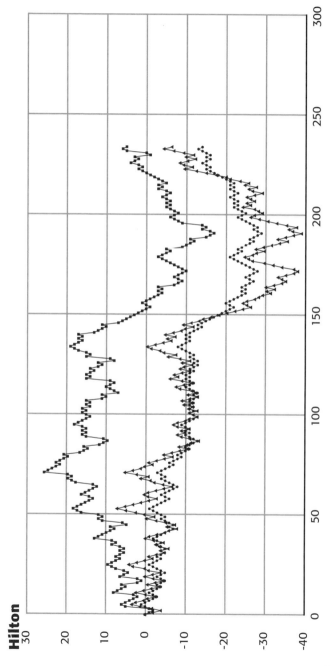

133

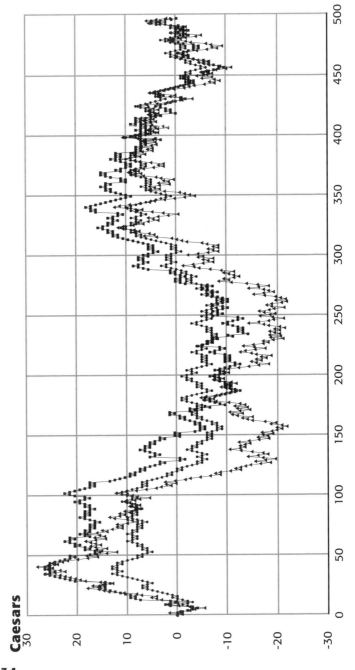

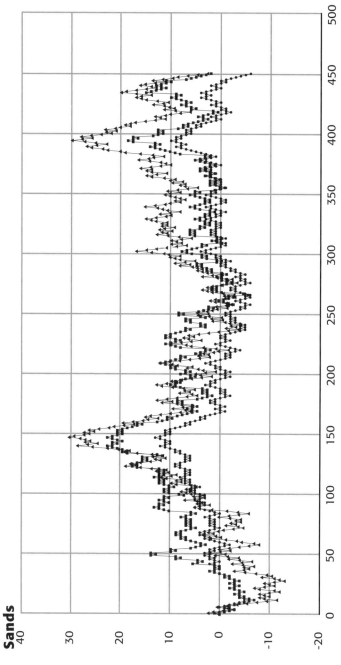

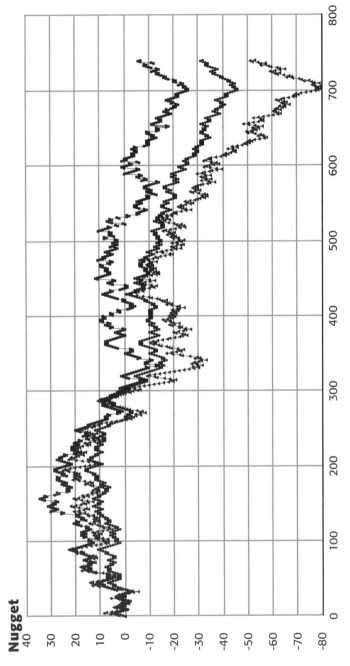

## Frontier

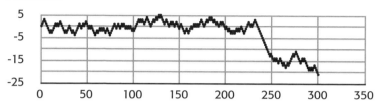

## Hilton

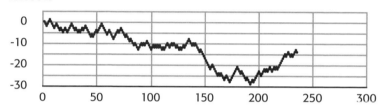

## Caesars

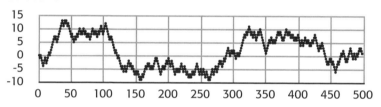

## Sands

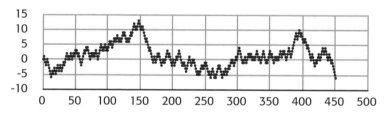

## Nugget

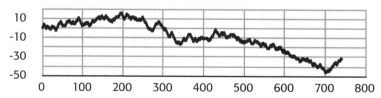

# EXAMINING THE EVIDENCE OF DICE CYCLING

After I had plotted my five hours of data from the Frontier and five hours of data from the Hilton, I was unable to see any definite evidence that any cycling was actually taking place. It was a fair assumption that the curve for the Frontier would turn upward, but there was no proof. I could speculate that if a cycle (from high to low to high) at the Frontier were to take 500 pass bet decisions from one high to the next high, it would show a drop between the two high points of seven (500 x 1.41%), thus forcing a probable upward motion of 18 from its last data point on the curve. However, if the curve were to stay at its present level of 25 below its high and sawtooth around this level for 1,800 points, the loss probability would also be satisfied (1,800 x 1.41%).

The Hilton curve tended to demonstrate the cycling theory. From the beginning, its direction had been down from a high of +1 to 28 units lower at -27 from where it had recovered upward for 13 units. Again the data was not conclusive. Therefore, I decided to record data for 10-hour intervals, which led to the curves for Caesars, the Sands, and the Nugget. The longer curves for Caesars, the Sands, and the Nugget give credibility to the cycling theory. All three show successive lows and highs.

After plotting the results for the Frontier, Hilton, Caesars, and the Sands and examining them, I noted the cumulative pass win motions moved upward from their lows somewhere between 16 and 20 units, and that the losses had downward motions somewhere between 21 and 25 units. When corrected for the dice number 12, this produced don't pass win motions between 16 and 21.

If these were the motion limits to which the dice would constantly closely adhere, winning at craps would be very simple. All you would have to do would be to determine, making small bets, where the highs and lows of this cycling occurred. Then you would increase the betting unit to a large one, followed by betting pass on the upward motions and don't pass on the downward ones.

A betting system like this would have been effective at the Frontier, Hilton, Caesars and the Sands, but what about the Nugget? It would have been a disaster at the Nugget! Although upward motions were limited to 16 at the Nugget, the cumulative don't pass motions fluctuated between 30 and 40, almost twice that of the other casinos. At the Nugget a change to pass betting after 16 or so don't pass wins would have led to losses which would have been much greater than the don't pass wins.

We must never forget that if something can happen at one crap table, it can also happen at all other crap tables. That is why a betting system such as this could have only spotty success.

# WHY A SYSTEM BASED ON HIGHS AND LOWS WOULD PRODUCE ONLY SPOTTY SUCCESS

If each single pass were immediately followed by a single loss, the performance curve would have a level saw-toothed pattern. If each larger consecutive pass group were to be immediately followed by a loss group of identical size, the performance curve would also have a level pattern, but with different size saw teeth. However, should the dice perform in either of these symmetrical ways, winning would be a certainty since all you would have to do is reverse your betting direction after completion of each group. Consequently, the dice must perform in unpredictable patterns if the casino is to profit from the guesswork of the players.

Therefore, instead of following level paths, the data plots of performance must curve upward and curve downward, and the surfaces of these lines must contain adjacent saw teeth of different sizes, and the lengths of these swings must also vary in order to give the casino a fighting chance.

For a performance line to curve upward it must contain more pass wins than loss decisions. Likewise, in order for it to curve downward, it must have more loss decisions than pass wins. The only way more pass wins can appear than loss decisions is through the production of consecutive pass wins. There cannot be an upward motion greater than one without a consecutive-pass group, and there cannot be a sizeable upward movement unless there is a sizeable number of more pass wins produced than loss decisions. This can happen *only* when the consecutive-pass-win groups are larger in size or number than the consecutive-loss groups that oppose them.

Between each pass-win group must be a loss group, and when the number of pass-wins produced by the consecutive pass-win groups is larger than the number of losses produced by the consecutive-loss groups, the motion will be upward. And when the number of losses produced by the consecutive loss groups is larger than the total pass wins in their separating consecutive-pass-win groups, the motion will be downward.

Each casino is represented by three curves. The ● ● ● ● curves are the same as those shown on page 137 and show the cumulative motion caused by single-unit pass bets. The ▲ ▲ ▲ ▲ curves show how the addition of pass odds bets on all points (pass and loss) would have affected the curve cycles. The ■ ■ ■ ■ curves show how the addition of parlaying bets on only the second pass bet decision of a hand, and only when the first pass bet decision had been a pass, would have further changed the range of the upward and downward movements.

In this latter case, if the first pass bet decision of a hand had been a crap, the second pass bet decision would not have been doubled. And neither would the third pass bet decision have been parlayed, even if the second pass bet decision in this case had been a pass. Only the second pass bet decision of a hand would ever have been doubled, and it would have been doubled *only* when the first pass bet decision of the hand had been a pass. Odds were also applied to these parlaying bets.

# MORE ON THE THIRD CURVE

Note that the third chart (■ ■ ■ ■ ■) looks at hands, as opposed to pass bet decisions. You only increase bets when the first pass bet decision in the hand wins. If the first pass bet decision loses, there will be no increase until the next hand begins, which must then meet the win-the-first pass bet decision criteria to increase the bet on the next pass bet. If that coming out roll is a loser—a 2, 3, or 12—you do not increase any bets.

We wait for the first pass win in a new hand. On this next pass bet, we double the size of the pass bet to 2 units. On the times that a point is established on the first roll—a 4, 5, 6, 8, 9, 10—you make an additional 2 unit pass odds bet. This extra bet, the odds bet, wins the same way the pass bet wins, by the point repeating before a 7 is thrown, and loses if a 7 is thrown before the point. The bets win and lose together. If the bets lose, you lose 2 units on the odds bet and 2 units on the pass. If the bet wins, it gets paid as follows:

| 2 UNIT ODDS BET PAYOFF | |
|---|---|
| POINT | WINNING RESULT |
| 4 or 10 | Wins 4 units |
| 5 or 9 | Wins 3 units |
| 6 or 8 | Wins 2.4 units |

These payoffs are in addition to the 2-unit even money win on the 2 unit pass bet.

If the bet wins and the hand is continued, you go back to the 1 unit pass bet with no odds. Note that in this system bets only doubles once per hand and odds are only placed on that doubled bet. Win or lose on that pass bet decision, the progression goes back to 1 unit with no odds bet. You only make the 2 unit bet—and then the odds if a point is established—after the first pass win as long as that win started the hand. If there is a second win, you go back to 1 unit with no odds. If the first pass bet decision in a hand loses, you wait for the next hand.

# PARLAYS AND SYSTEMS

There are an infinite number of ways odds bets, the parlaying of bets, and the combining of all these bets can be applied. The arrangements used for these curves were selected because of their simplicity. They clearly show the effect that each of these betting factors imposes on overall results.

When we view these curves, it becomes obvious that in each case, the size of the movements of the cumulative wins and the sizes of the movements of the cumulative losses *increase* with each new betting application, whether it is odds bets or whether it is the parlaying of bets.

We can glean from this that when we're betting pass, we should apply the use of odds and the parlaying of bets if we are to obtain the largest winnings—but these should be applied *only* when the dice are in an upward motion. When the dice are in a downward cycle, the losses will be greatly increased by adding odds and parlaying to our bets.

# WHAT WE CAN LEARN FROM THE CURVES

From these curves we can form some very general limits as to sizes of the upward and downward movements.

1. Upward movements with unit pass bets will net out at a 16-unit to 20-unit profit.
2. Upward movements with unit pass bets combined with unit odds bets will net out at a 30-unit to 35-unit profit.
3. Upward movements with unit pass bets combined with odds bets, with double-unit pass bets, and with double-unit odds bets on the second decisions of hands when the first decision has been a win will net out at a 40-unit to 45-unit profit.
4. Downward movements with unit pass bets will net out at a 21-unit to 25-unit loss.
5. Downward movements with unit pass bets combined with unit odds bets will net out at a 40-unit to 45-unit loss.
6. Downward movements with unit pass bets combined with odds bets, with double-unit pass bets, and with double-unit odds bets on the second decision of hands when the first point has been a win will net out a 45-unit to 60-unit loss.

# REASONABLE EXPECTATIONS

The conclusions we have drawn for the cycling limits for the three betting schemes were very general. All five casinos supported the upward movement limits. The first four supported the downward movement limits, but the Nugget far exceeded the downward movements of the other four casinos.

However, since all the casinos agreed at some time with their upward movements, it would have been possible to have obtained a 40-unit profit at each casino.

The following examples show what a 40-unit profit would mean.

1. If the betting unit were $5, this would mean a $200 win, and if this were realized each day, the yearly income would be $73,000.
2. If the betting unit were $25, the daily win would be $1,000, and the yearly income rate would be $365,000.
3. If the betting unit were $100, the yearly income rate would be $1,460,000.

Now, let's ask some questions.

1. How many $5-chip bettors realize $73,000 of spending money each year from their salaries and other incomes?
2. How many $25-chip bettors realize $365,000 of spending money each year from their salaries and other income?
3. How many $100-chip bettors realize $1,460,000 of spending money each year from their salaries and other incomes?

Let's ask some more questions:

1. How many $5-chip bettors would be satisfied with winning only $200 after spending three or four hours at a crap table?
2. How many $25-chip bettors have the limited ambition of winning only $1,000 for three or four hours work at a crap table?

3. How many $100-chip bettors have their sights set as low as $4,000 for each three or four hours of crap playing?
4. And last but not least, how many $5-chip, $25-chip, and $100-chip players can limit themselves to making only pass bets—and can refrain from dabbling with the sucker bets?

We cannot say for certain that a 40-unit win for a three or four-hour stint at a crap table is a reasonable expectation. It could be less than this, but it certainly would not be a great deal more. Unfortunately, very few weekend gamblers could limit themselves to as small a win as 40 units and be satisfied with their performances.

A crap player is not only just anxious to win, he is greedy! He not only wants to bet on every roll so as to win big in a hurry, but he also does *not* wish to miss even one small opportunity to win. He is never satisfied with a small, reasonable profit. He wants it all!

> Most crap players aren't satisfied with a small profit. This weakness leads to sucker bets, bad money management, and losses. Avoid this losing syndrome.

It is this greediness that fuels his desire to far exceed a reasonable return and forces him to make bets where odds are stacked heavily against him. Only on rare occasions does such foolishness pay a reward.

## WHEN CAN WE WIN?

The curves on pages 132 through 136 showed us that placing odds on pass bets and letting the pass bets double will greatly increase the winning totals during the upward movements of the dice. This will also increase the losses during downward movements.

Naturally, being able to realize 40 pass units of profit consistently requires the ability to select when the dice have embarked on a winning course and to be able to recognize when the dice have run out of upward steam. Unfortunately, there is no mathematically precise way for predicting when these upward movements will commence—but there are many signs that will appear to signal that the dice are heading downward. This may sound like a negative approach to winning, but it is the best I have.

The purpose of this book is not to show you how to win through big fantasies. Its purpose is to instruct you on how to be successful at craps. The certain way to be unsuccessful is to continue to bet pass during down motions.

We must get out when downward movements commence, even if we have a loss!

## FOLLOW YOUR BRAIN'S DIRECTIONS

To understand these signals, we must recognize the human brain is an instinctively accurate computer. Your brain is far superior to any electronic computer whose abilities depend entirely on how it had been mathematically programmed.

Your brain can pick up signals that you have not yet consciously recognized. Because of this, if at any time you feel strongly uncomfortable with a betting direction, you should either decrease your betting unit to a comfortable size, or stop betting until you feel comfortable again.

Every brain at the crap table is subconsciously correlating and analyzing results of each dice roll. A player is unaware of what the brain's evaluations are leading to until the brain transmits a strong danger signal making the bettor very uncomfortable with his present betting direction. His reaction to such a strong uncomfortable feeling should be to either decrease his betting unit or stop betting. Instead, this fear signal often triggers the bettor to panic bet—that's when he places large desperate bets trying to recover losses. He often leaves place bets riding far longer than he should. He will also do other foolish things before becoming discouraged and leaving the table. But leave the table he will! This is the self-accepted sign that the dice have turned against him.

When a lot of players start leaving a crap table, it is a clear signal that the dice have peaked and are on a downswing. People exit a crap table because of frustration and disappointment over their inability to win. Long before this exodus begins, smiles have disappeared and players start cursing to themselves as they fight their subconscious signal to quit. Their brains have picked up quit signals from other players and have related them correctly with the downward performance of the dice.

But players are often slow to grasp these warnings. Most people have one common fault—they think they're smarter than their subconscious brain.

## WHAT CAUSES FRUSTRATION AT CRAP TABLES?

Most losing frustrations at crap tables are caused by the failure of the sucker bets to pay profits. During winning movements, the sucker bets, like the pass bets, yield winnings. During losing movements, sucker bets get chopped off quickly. Let's see why this happens.

During winning movements, there must be a fair number of consecutive passes. During losing movements, there must be consecutive losses. To this, we could say, "So what?"

It looks like a standoff, but there is a great difference between consecutive passes and consecutive losses.

When a consecutive-pass group occurs, this group must have its beginning and ending during the same hand by the same roller. There is no way that consecutive passes can be continued from one roller's hand into the next roller's hand because there must be a loss decision ending with a 7 and thus separating the two hands. On the other hand, a consecutive loss group can have as many rollers participate in it as the number of consecutive losses.

For example, during the 40 hours at the five casinos, there were six times when eight passes were rolled consecutively. A total of only six individuals were involved in rolling them. There was one case where 16 losses were rolled consecutively. About this we can say nothing definite except that as many as 16 rollers could have been involved, or as few as one roller. This latter, of course, would be very doubtful because for one roller to have accomplished this, he would needed to have rolled 15 consecutive craps followed by a losing decision ending with a 7. This fantasy might happen sometime during the next 4,000 years! Actually, 14 rollers were involved in this 16 consecutive-loss group, as two of the hands had two losses that occurred because they were started with craps.

## HOW DO CONSECUTIVE PASSES OR LOSSES AFFECT SUCKER BETTORS?

This difference between the number of hands participating in consecutive losses and the one hand producing consecutive passes greatly affects the fortunes of bettors playing place bets and other sucker bets. When consecutive pass points are rolled, the place bets and the other sucker bets are transferred from the rolls of one pass bet decision in the hand into the rolls of the following pass bet decision in the same hand.

Complete losses occur only with the concluding 7 of the last decision of the hand. Consequently, only one major loss occurs—that is, assuming that the bettor has listened to the "friendly" dealer and has been off when any coming out 7's were rolled. Therefore, if the hand has been a long one with a great number of rolls, the place bettor has probably withdrawn a large part of his winnings so that the last roll does not hurt too deeply, leaving him with a small profit.

When consecutive losses involve a number of different players, the place bets and other sucker bets are wiped out at the conclusion of each hand, which is usually after only a few rolls of the dice. As a result, a place-and-sucker bettor can have his winnings *and* his bankroll wiped out rapidly by a few consecutive loss hands. Why? Because each new hand requires the sucker bettor to come up with new betting money.

We have already discussed why a sucker bettor should parlay his sucker bets in order to maximize his winnings during winning movements. However, few sucker bettors ever do this to any great degree and therefore, their winnings are only a fraction of what they should be. As a result, they are very vulnerable to failure and frustration when a losing movement is in its first stages because their winning bankrolls are so much smaller than they should be. This expedites their quick failures and speedy exodus early in a down movement far in advance of the bottom of the movement.

# WATCH THE PLAYERS
# AND THE DICE

A pass-oriented bettor must train himself to leave the table at the beginning of the sucker-bettor exodus if he wants to be successful—*and* he must be able to ascertain when this exodus is starting. You should constantly study what the other players at the table are doing to judge how they are faring. And you should be as aware of the numbers and movements of players to and away from the table as you are aware of what the dice are doing.

At Caesars, the table became empty seven times during the 10 hours I spent in the casino. I was interested in seeing whether the dice would continue on their same paths after these interruptions so I didn't attempt to keep them rolling by throwing them myself during any of this down time. When we study the data and look at the charts for Caesars, we cannot see any evidence to indicate anything other than that the dice took up their directions at the same place as they had been when play had stopped.

One of the down times was an hour in length. The total for all down times was two hours and 40 minutes, leaving only seven hours and 40 minutes of actual dice-rolling time. If we project the pass bet decision-production rate that was present during the seven hours and 20 minutes to 10 hours of rolling time, the total number of pass bet decisions would have been about 700, which would have put Caesars' total pass bet decisions close to those of the Nugget. Like the Nugget, Caesars rarely had more than a few players at the table at any time. Because of this, dealers were able to resolve the distribution of all betting chips quickly and keep the dice moving when players were at the table.

# WHAT CAUSES PLAYERS TO LEAVE A CRAP TABLE?

Let's examine what the conditions were when the table at Caesars first went empty. This first complete exodus took place after the 49th pass bet decision was concluded after I had joined the table.

On the 41st pass bet decision, the dice had hit a high movement of +17 (single-unit pass bets), +31.3 (single-unit pass bets with unit odds bets), and +30.4 (single-unit pass bets, odds bets, doubling bets on second pass). The 49th decision happened only eight decisions later during a declining movement when everyone at the table had become discouraged. At that time the score had fallen and stood at +11, +21.3, and +22.0, respectively. The actual exodus began several points before this 49th roll at a time when the winnings were higher.

Following the first complete flight of players, the table never attracted more than a few players at any time. It took only a short run of losses to discourage all of them. After the last roll at 2 a.m., the table went empty again. This was rather surprising since the dice had been performing fairly well.

At the Nugget, the table went empty except for me and another player who would not throw the dice, after the 271st pass bet decision. The score at this time stood at -3.0, -8.4, and 2.0 for the three betting conditions. Seventy-seven points before, it stood at +19, +30.5, and +36.6. The players began to desert the table many pass bet decisions before the final exodus at the 271st pass bet decision. The first deserters left when the profits were still high. When this lack of rollers appeared at the 271st decision, I rolled the dice to keep the data coming. I had to roll three hands in a row before new players, willing to roll the dice, joined the table. During these three hands, I produced 17 pass bet decisions, one of which was a crap. There were the three pass losses with 7's that ended the hands, and 13 of the pass bet decisions were pass winners.

In the first hand, I had eight consecutive passes, which made it one of the six eight-consecutive-pass groups encountered in the 40 hours, and one of the three at the Nugget. In this first hand, during this eight-consecutive-pass performance, I rolled 7 four consecutive times, which was one of the six "four-consecutive-7" groups produced during the 40 hours, as well as one of the three "four-consecutive-7" groups rolled at the Nugget. I rolled the dice 44 times and had nine 7's, which is a ratio of one 7 for each five rolls.

During the first hand in which there were nine pass wins, there were only 11 rolls of the dice which would have made place bet returns, assuming the place bets were always off on the coming out rolls. Despite the nine pass wins and the eight consecutive passes, this was not a hot hand. The sucker bettors would have had little to cheer about.

And, despite this net upward movement of nine (13 pass wins less four losses), these three hands produced only a large sawtooth in the downward movement that had started 77 pass bet decisions earlier. One productive run of dice such as this does not necessarily commence a change in dice direction. But when a direction reversal of a magnitude such as this occurs, it takes resolve not to change your betting direction!

> Craps is the one casino game whose patterns can be studied without having the studies cancelled by a change of dice, change of tables, or change from one honest casino to another honest one.

# DON'T PASS ANALYSIS

We concentrated our discussions of betting entirely upon the pass betting side. The downward movements have been pass losses, not don't pass wins.

If we reverse our analysis to placing all our bets on the don't pass side, we would arrive at similar conclusions to those arrived at with pass betting. They are:

1. Unit don't pass bets produce the lowest winnings.
2. Unit don't pass bets with odds (free odds bets) produce higher winnings.
3. Doubling the second bet of an odds series after the first don't pass bet decision was a don't pass winner would produce the highest return.

The don't pass analysis would parallel the pass analysis except for one very important factor—there would be no signal as to when the motion of the dice would be changing from winning to losing. After the dice had produced several consecutive don't pass losses, a player would never be able to rationalize whether these were merely negative sawtooths in a winning cycle or the beginning of a losing direction. He would have to rely entirely upon guesswork. For this reason, if for no other, a bettor should study and concentrate on pass betting. People tend to leave a crap table when a winning pass direction reverses, but do not flock toward a table when a winning don't pass direction reverses.

Another factor against don't pass betting is that the table might go empty of players after only a few winning don't pass bet decisions, thus leaving the don't pass bettor without rollers to provide winning rolls for him. Rarely does an exodus of players start during a winning pass motion. Consequently, the pass bettor can carry his betting to a conclusion, whereas the don't pass bettor is often denied this opportunity.

Our next discussion revolves around a question people have often asked me: What difference does it make whether I gamble in a home craps game or take my action to a casino? Using the data we've discussed in-depth in the preceding chapters, let's try to find the best answer to that question.

# 12 FOUR RULES TO FOLLOW IN PASS DECISIONS

Our discussions and data have concluded that a crap player will have better control over his fortune betting *with* the dice (pass) than *against* the dice (don't pass)—even though the return ratio for either direction is the same, 98.59%.

Now, let us establish the rules that our discussions and data dictate that a crap player should follow with the pass direction, starting with selecting which crap table to play.

## 1. SELECT THE RIGHT CRAP TABLE

The selection of the table is the most important decision for starting a possible winning experience. In the previous chapter we discussed signs that signal the beginning of a losing cycle. These signs were based upon the assumption that the player already had been at the table and enjoying a winning movement for a fair period of time. However, when you first enter a casino, you do not have this experience to guide you. You have many no-nos, but barely one yes.

The following discussions are aimed at helping you select a table where you might be rewarded with a winning movement.

(a) Never go to an empty table. The table is empty either because a downward movement has chased all its players away or because it is just opening

**155**

---

for the day. If it is just opening, you should have knowledge about what the action of the dice were when it closed the evening before, because today's beginning movement will be a continuation of yesterday's closing movement.

The dice on a crap table, we must remember, are constantly attempting to balance themselves with their probabilities. The chances are that a table opening for the first time today, closed on a downward movement yesterday, chasing away its last players when there were few players left in the casino.

**(b)** This naturally initiates the question, "Who should open an empty table?" It is customary for the house to use shills who are paid by the casino to bet at empty tables so that it appears that the table is active. Shills are most necessary at small casinos where there are fewer customers. Shills are identified rather easily since they usually make minimum bets, show little emotion, and drift away from tables without apparent reason when customers begin to arrive. There is nothing wrong with shills rolling the dice and having them speed up completion of a losing movement so dice may change to a winning one. If shills are posted around the table, wait for them to leave, and then observe whether legitimate players are staying before you enter the game.

**(c)** If a table is crowded with players, it is quite possible that it has been enjoying a winning movement. It is also quite possible that this winning movement might be topping out.

**(d)** If a table is enjoying a hot hand with much cheering and excitement, it might be fun to watch the action, but when it ends there is no way of determining whether this hot hand had taken place at the beginning, middle or end of an upward movement. Players who have won heavily and have recovered a good part of their previous losses often leave the table to cash in and enjoy some moments of prosperity with folding money in their pocket. They eventually will return to the battlefield to lose it, but they like the temporary feeling of wealth that folding money gives them.

(e) A table half full with players is a fair prospect. Watch it for a few hands. Observe whether players are leaving or staying. If they are staying, take a place at the table. Do not hesitate to ask the player next to you how the dice have been doing. If his answer is "lousy" and you've noticed that no one has been leaving the table, ask someone else. Get a second opinion. If you next receive a "so, so" or a "not bad," or a "pretty good," you have struck a fair prospect. If the dice have been performing in a level pattern, you have a way of betting that could produce winnings. At least your losses should not be heavy, and you may be present for the next upward movement of the dice at the table.

I always like a half-filled crap table more than a crowded or empty one. It was probably my instinctive choice of such tables that led me to observe what appeared to be cycling of the movements of the dice, because I usually started by winning, followed by losing, then followed by panic betting and large losses. In selecting my tables for collecting the data for this book, I was naturally attracted by these same table conditions. It is interesting to observe that all five tables first produced winning returns before downward movements began.

(f) If you fail to find a casino table that you feel comfortable with, go to another casino. Don't buck your intuitions!

# 2. MAKE PROPER BETS

You may wish to begin betting with a smaller unit bet than the one you want to employ as your long-term betting unit. It is good policy for you to begin with a small betting unit and not increase it until you begin to feel comfortable at the table. However, you should always use the odds bets and the doubling-bet system even with this small unit of betting. A $2 odds bet, which requires an original $2 pass bet, can be placed on 4's and 10's and on 5's and 9's. If 6 or 8 is the point, odds bets can be simulated by placing a $2 bet on 6 or 8, whichever is the point.

You should continue betting in the pass direction until receiving definite signs that the dice have reversed downward. There will be times when you encounter consecutive losses and these reduce your winnings considerably. But in order to be a winner, you must have courage enough to carry your betting direction to a conclusion.

If, at times during your upward-movement betting, you become uncomfortable and feel questionable about your direction even though no signs of a downturn have been signaled, either reduce your betting unit to a comfortable size, or stop betting until your confidence returns.

> It's so important I'm going to remind you of the two no-no's: Never attempt to recover your losses by placing large bets or reversing your betting direction.

When you're playing at a table where the dice are performing in an upward movement, you should scan the casino and observe action at other tables. Eventually the dice at your table will reverse and you'll want to switch tables to continue. The rules for selecting a new table are exactly the same as for selecting the first table, except that in this case, you've had several hours to observe before you must make a decision.

# 3. GREED AND PANIC

Perhaps the most defeating instinct that people have is greed. People always want more of the things they have, and rarely are satisfied relinquishing some and settling for less.

Years ago, during the latter part of the Great Depression, a stockbroker friend explained to me how greed affected most people. It seemed that this broker had a customer who entered the stock market with $10,000 and, through the broker's advice and application of margin, increased his paper value to $30,000. The market then reversed and the customer's account dropped to $20,000—still $10,000 higher than his original investment.

Seeing signs that the market would drop further, the broker advised him to sell and take his $10,000 profit.

"No," said his customer. "I have a $10,000 loss, not a $10,000 profit. I'll sell only when I get my $10,000 back."

Needless to say, the market fell, and the customer's value fell to where he finally lost everything and wound up losing his original $10,000.

Most crap addicts reason the way this stock market customer did. When the dice reverse and winnings decrease, instead of heeding signals around them, their greed promotes panic betting as the vehicle to recoup their losses. The result?

They not only lose their winnings, they lose more additional money.

> You must recognize warning signals and leave the game whether you are winning or losing. Throwing good money after bad will bring certain disaster.

# 4. STUDY THE GAME TO BE SUCCESSFUL

To be consistently successful at anything, a person must constantly study his subject to keep up to date. This is especially true of craps. We try something today and it works. We try it tomorrow and it fails. Unless we have complete data showing how the dice performed during both times, we cannot study why we succeeded one time and failed the next. For this reason, a serious crap player should record all dice rolls, then tabulate the data to analyze it. Unless he does this, he won't learn from his mistakes. He will always be guessing and be continually frustrated by his failures. And he probably will be prone to gamble foolishly through attempts at quick recoveries.

The biggest handicap that each of us faces is our own self. Many pilots have flown their aircraft into mountains because they failed to believe their flight instruments. Unfortunately, they never got a second chance to study where they went wrong. The best way we can learn how to believe signals, our playing instruments, at the crap table is having an accurate record of what occurred.

Many of us have made thousands of rolls of the dice. Some of us have also developed the impression that our personal shooting of the dice is different from those that other shooters experience—but are they? Can we really know unless we have data to substantiate such impressions? Perhaps our successes have overshadowed our losses in our memories. Perhaps the reverse is true. We can only get an accurate picture of our personal dice throwing effectiveness by collecting complete data each time we roll the dice. Knowledge about our own crap shooting history can provide us with some good opportunities for successful betting.

I used a small ring notebook in collecting my data. Holding this notebook in my left hand and recording each roll caused no problem with my betting or dice rolling. If you use a similar method of recording data, you may want to note hands where you rolled the dice, and initial the side of each hand you rolled. You can use side borders for recording notes like time or number of players at the table, or other data you consider relevant.

While I was transferring my notebook data to data sheets, I automatically noticed many dice patterns I thought worthy of study. For example, there were 36 pass bet decision lines on each data sheet, the exact number as the number of dice combinations present with a pair of dice. Consequently, I soon found myself computing the quantities of the different dice numbers rolled on the 36 coming out rolls, because from these I could get a fairly accurate impression of how closely dice had actually followed their probabilities.

I noticed that the last line on most data sheets consisted of a losing point with a 7. Out of curiosity, I totaled these and found that 36 of the 59 sheets with all their 36 lines filled with pass bet decisions had losing pass bet decisions on their last lines with a point and with a concluding 7. In addition, five more last lines contained losers with craps, totaling 41 losers to 18 winners.

Since none of the craps were 12's (although theoretically there should have been one or two of them), if a bet of don't pass had been placed on the 36th coming out roll and on each

multiple of 36 following the first one at each casino, a profit of 23 units would have been realized during the 40 hours of crap play. This, of course, is basically trivia. Certainly there are no probability calculations that would lead to any such betting scheme. Probability says that for 59 coming out rolls, there should be 30 losing pass bet decisions and 29 winning ones for the pass bettor. For the don't pass bettor, there should be 29 losing ones and 28 winners, since two of the coming out rolls should be no-decision 12's.

The fact that the score stood at a loss of 23 units after the 59 coming out rolls instead of at a loss of one unit *does* demonstrate one important fact about the game of craps: The decisions in the game fluctuate in cycles around their norms. Therefore, if we follow and make a data record of the 36 coming out multiples at each casino we visit for our next thousand or so hours, we could expect the direction of the pass bet decisions to reverse and follow an upward path at some point.

Obviously a cyclical betting system built around events which would occur only on each 36th pass bet decision, even though it might be successful, would be very time consuming and of low profit, regardless what the betting unit was. To be successful in craps, we must search for cyclical betting decisions of much shorter time spans.

The first number rolled at the first casino, the Frontier, was a hardway 4. Since this gave an immediate hardway 4 win, I was curious about how betting on hardway 4 would cycle, so I studied the hardway 4 production at the Frontier with the following results:

If there had been a one-unit bet always riding on the hardway 4 on every roll including all the coming out ones, and if the profits had been picked up when each hardway 4 had been rolled, during the 29th pass bet decision when a hardway 4 was thrown, the total profit at that time would have been 38 units.

After 80 pass bet decisions later, the score would have stood at an overall loss of five units.

During the next 160 pass bet decisions, there would have been an upward movement of 52 units yielding a net overall position of 47 units of profit.

Thirty pass bet decisions later, which brought the evening to a close at the Frontier, resulted in a downward motion of six, thus giving a final tally of 41 units profit for having kept a unit bet working on hardway 4 on every roll of the dice at the Frontier.

Instead of withdrawing the seven-unit winnings each time a hardway 4 appeared, suppose the bet had been parlayed and winnings removed only after consecutive double wins. In that case, during the 29th pass bet decision, the profit would have stood at 108 units. After 94 pass bet decisions later, the net winnings would have declined by 66 to a 42 profit level, after which they would have begun to rise, so that during the 51st pass bet decision later, they would have risen to net winnings of 205 units. After 125 pass bet decisions, which would have included the last pass bet decision during the evening at the Frontier, the final net winnings would have declined to 104.

When betting the hardway 4, if the player had been listening to the "friendly expert" dealer and, as a result, had not had his bets working on the coming out rolls, his overall profit when removing all his winnings after each hardway 4 would have been 10 units less at 31 units. If he had been parlaying his bets to double while having them off on the coming out rolls, his profit for the night would have been 73 units less, with a final total of 31 units profit instead of 104.

The fact that a profit would have resulted at the Frontier if a player had bet hardway 4 blindly on each roll does not mean that such betting will produce a profit or even come close to producing a profit the next time.

The foregoing examples demonstrate that cycling is present in all the betting opportunities the casino table offers. Therefore, there are times when concentrated betting on any of these will produce winnings. However, you must also realize that the overall results at casinos will also cycle. Therefore, your returns will also cycle, and in the end you will show an overall loss if you continue to always bet the identical way each time you go to a crap table.

> Your ability to adjust to the way a table performs is the key to beating the game of craps.

I am not suggesting that you concentrate on a hardway 4 betting scheme. My purpose here is to show you that the casino crap table can offer many different betting opportunities that might be successful if played correctly. Without doubt, you can develop a great many of them. The example of the hardway 4 simply demonstrates a procedure you can follow to study the dice. It can be used when developing many of the possible betting schemes that we can conceive.

The purpose of this book is to educate, not dictate!

Constant study is what leads to success. This entails the constant collection of actual crap table data. There is only one way that you will acquire the actual data under which you performed at the crap table: You must record it yourself. Fortunately, craps is a game that lends itself to easy record-keeping. Blackjack, on the other hand, is one game where it is practically impossible to record each card dealt. A person can keep track of roulette wheel results by recording every number as they occur, but the house can make all this research obsolete by changing wheels.

# 13 HOME GAME OR CASINO CRAPS?

The basic game of craps provides a 98.59% return. This represents far less risk than practically any business venture—and yet, many bettors produce a 0% return on craps.

The return for every crap player could be 98.59%, provided that each player bet either pass and come, or don't pass and don't come on every roll of the dice. Yet many bettors make a fewer number of bets than these would require, and thus manage to accomplish much lower returns.

A U.S. senate committee, for lack of anything important to discuss, investigated the game of craps back in 1957. They concluded that the casino's take from the money bet at crap tables was 24%. John Scarne, a former consultant for the casino operations of the Hilton Hotels, says a casino's take is 20%.

In tabulating the return ratios for all the bets offered on a crap table, we know that the lowest return ratio was 83.33% and the highest was 99.54%. This means that if a player were to play any one particular bet with consistency, the casino's take should be less than 20%.

The reason casinos have this 20% (Scarne) or 24% (senate committee) income is because players misplay their bets! For example, they do not parlay their sucker bets, and thus put themselves into bets whose return ratios are much lower than 80%. Further, players panic and then attempt to recover their losses by placing large bets after the dice have reversed against

their betting directions. In brief, most crap players have not taken the time necessary to study the game of craps. They bet from an ignorant point of view.

A person who enters the automobile manufacturing business or any other business would certainly spend time studying the risks involved before investing. He knows that if his knowledge is limited or incomplete, his chances for success will be poor. Though playing for years, most crap players have managed to acquire only a superficial knowledge of the game. If you have been one of them, I hope this book will help turn things around for you.

# THE FADING GAME

Even though the odds are 1,004 to 976 against a roller making a pass—thus having the dice apparently favoring the fade bettor by offering him a possible 101.41% return ratio—a player's best chance to come out ahead in a single evening's private game of craps comes with his rolling the dice.

The reason? The 1,004 to 976 odds are based on the assumption that the bettor will bet the same unit bet against the dice on each coming out roll. In the fading game, the bettor does not have the certainty of being able to bet the same unit against the dice on each coming out roll. Why? Because players on his left, with the opportunity to fade all or a part of the offerings of the bettors on their lefts, may not leave anything for him to fade against. They may also leave less for him to fade than his desired unit bet.

Whether dice are thrown on a casino crap table or on the floor in a fading game, the basic structure of the pass bet decisions and hands will be the same. There will be short decisions and long decisions. There will be craps, 7's and 11's on the coming out rolls, and there will be "hot hands."

On the casino table, "hot hands" are those that produce a large number of dice rolls, therefore producing good winning results for the sucker bettors cheering loudly at each non-7 roll. In the fading game, "hot hands" are those producing a large number of passes, preferably consecutively. On a casino table, a large number of non-7 rolls could be produced in a hand having only a few passes, thus producing a hot hand for sucker bettors. A large number of rolls in a fading game merely eat time on the way to a pass's conclusion.

At the Frontier Hotel, we had a run of 16 consecutive losses. Had a bettor allowed a $1 bet to parlay as don't pass bets for the 16 consecutive losses, he could theoretically have won $65,529. Had these 16-consecutive losses occurred in a fading game, there would not have been any way for a bettor to have benefited more than slightly by betting against the dice. As dice passed to the left through the hands of 14 shooters, so would the fading of the shooters' bets have been passing to the left, with no opportunity for parlaying a don't bet. As a result, the final tally probably would have been virtually a standoff, with each player losing on his roll and winning when he faded the next shooter's roll.

The opportunity for parlaying his bets lies with the shooter in the fading game. When he has a hot hand with a run of consecutive passes, he can permit bets to multiply by offering the entire winning pots for other players to fade against. This is the only way a player in the fading game can produce large winnings from a small bet.

Whether on the casino table or on the floor in a fading game, dice follow similar cyclical patterns and produce similar pass hands with the same number of consecutive passes. In the fading game, since the only time the rolling of the dice will be stopped is after the completion of each pass bet decision, the number of rolls will be high; and consequently, the number of pass bet decisions rolled will also be high.

Let's compare the performance of the dice in a fading game with that of the casino game at the Nugget where dice moved rapidly. At the Nugget, there were three hands with eight consecutive passes, one hand with seven consecutive passes, two hands with six, four hands with five, 18 hands with four, and 19 hands with three. In a fading game, similar results should occur. So, it is fairly certain each of us as a shooter should experience several of these—maybe not one of the eight, seven, or six consecutive passes, but surely some of the others. Now, if we can refrain from betting against any of these other "hot hands" by letting the eager beavers on our right cover at each of our turns—and if we play our shooting hands so as to capitalize to the fullest on our "hot" ones—we should do fairly well. And if one of the "very hot hands" comes our way, we should win big.

## IS THERE A FORMULA FOR BETTING IN THE FADING GAME?

No. There is no set formula that can be applied on how to bet when rolling the dice in a fading game. A shooter must do what he is comfortable doing. For example, he may feel best by withdrawing his original bet after making a pass on his first pass bet before letting his bets parlay. He may prefer playing for two passes before withdrawing part of it. The shooter must decide this for himself. But one thing is certain: When a hot hand comes along, if the shooter does not make the most of it by letting his bets multiply, he is not going to be a big winner.

Along with other authors, Scarne disagrees with my contention that the way to win in the private crap game is by rolling the dice. Scarne uses the odds of 1,004 to 976 against passing as one reason. He then elaborates by giving examples of the odds chiseler who makes side bets the suckers buy. For example, when a 4 is rolled on the coming out roll, an odds chiseler might offer 4 to 1 odds that the shooter will not make his point with a hardway 4, instead of offering the correct odds of 8 to 1.

But are the odds always 8 to 1 against rolling a hardway 4? If the coming out roll had been a hardway 4, odds against the point being made with a hardway 4 are 62 to 1, not 8 to 1 because the bet is actually a bet against having the shooter roll two consecutive hardway 4's, not just one. In this case the odds chiseler is really chiseling.

How many times have we heard friendly dealers suggest hardway bets when the point has just been established by a hardway number? The odds chiseler in the fading game is not the only person who practices odds chiseling!

The best protection a crap player has against an odds chiseler is to first remember not to accept any of his bets and, second, to expose him by asking him to offer correct odds and then tell him what they are.

A major purpose of this book is to inform you what the odds and return ratios are so that you won't be victimized. However, odds chiseling is not the only method used for bilking innocents in the private game. This is why *Scarne on Dice* is must reading for all crap players.

# THE ADVANTAGES OF PLAYING CRAPS IN A CASINO GAME

The casino table offers the crap addict the opportunity for completely controlling the amounts he bets. It gives him the privilege of betting as though he were the shooter on each coming out roll, not just when he is the shooter as in the fading game. The casino table also permits him to bet against the dice if he is so inclined. The casino table gives the crap addict the privilege of playing the game his own way—and the privilege of losing his own way.

# CROOKED GAMES

One book that every crap player should read is *Scarne on Dice* by John Scarne, which is represented as being "everything anyone would ever want to know about dice and dice games." I take exception to this claim, because Scarne does not go any deeper into the game of craps than any other author. As a result, he comes to many of the same wrong conclusions about the game as many other authors.

The exceptions I take toward any of Scarne's conclusions are not meant to reflect a derogatory opinion of his abilities. However, I feel certain that if Scarne had dug as deeply into the research of casino craps as I have done, he would have arrived at the same conclusions—in which case, there would have been no reason for me to write this book.

Scarne is recognized as the world's authority on crooked dice and dice manipulation. During World War II he acted as the gambling advisor to the United States Armed Forces, not just with dice but with all gambling games. If for no other reason, crap players should read his book to learn the many ways that dishonest players in illegal games can manipulate odds to their favor. Scarne concentrates on the use of loaded and other crooked dice, and on controlled dice rolling. He says that for you to get a fair shake with craps, you should only patronize casinos that have proven their integrity by being large and by having been in business for a long time because casinos do not need to manipulate the dice in order to survive.

The discussions of craps and the probabilities that I present in this book are based only on what will occur with honest dice in honest casinos (and with honest dice and honest players in private games). Discussions of dishonest dice in shady casinos and in crooked private games are left to Scarne.

# SUCKER BETS...AGAIN

If you cannot refrain from dabbling in sucker bets, you should make it a firm rule never to speculate in them except with winnings. In other words, you should play these bets only with "house money" and never with "frightened money."

When you speculate with a sucker bet, you should play it to maintain its highest return ratio. Either give your money the maximum chance of multiplying by parlaying all winnings immediately on the same sucker bet, or remove your bet and your winnings after your first win.

When you feel uncomfortable with your sucker bets, remove all of them. The percent return on the sucker bets is poor at best. The percent return becomes very, very poor when the sucker bets are played incorrectly.

# THE LANGUAGE OF CRAPS

Craps is the most exciting game in the casino. A blind man can find a crap table in a crowded casino merely by listening for the raucous comments and cheering that crap players emit at every roll of the dice. Craps has a distinctive language all its own.

"Baby needs a new pair of shoes!"

"Read 'em and weep!"

"Come seven or eleven!"

"Little Joe!"

Law enforcement officers can easily locate and shut down illegal crap games being played in back alleys and other hidden places by lurking in the shadows near likely locations and listening for these telltale sounds.

The boisterous language of craps has passed from illegal floating games to public casinos, which have introduced new exclamations such as "Hardway 8!" Crap players also moan incoherently in defeat, and they cheer raucously for a hand well rolled. Much like the flame that attracts a moth, these noises eventually attract the attention of inexperienced gamblers— and it won't be long before they burn their wings in the bright excitement of the crap table. You do not need to be one of them!

# 14    **LAST WORD**

If you expected this book to lead you into Fantasyland and keep you there with promises of instant wealth—or if you expected to find the secret to spending a weekend in Las Vegas or Atlantic City and win enough money to instantly retire—you are no doubt disappointed.

The purpose of this book has not changed from the title on its cover to its last words. I wrote it to guide you to smarter craps strategy while giving you a more intelligent, insider view of the game.

And perhaps during our travels through statistics, and data, and probabilities, maybe—just maybe—you've grown to love the game of craps as much as I do!

# 15 ONE MORE THOUGHT

### AN AFTERTHOUGHT ON HOW TO BEAT
### THE CASINO AT ITS OWN GAME

There is no mathematical way to make bets on a crap table that result in a sure thing for the bettor. But there is a way to bet that can reap a profit from the casino every time you try it. A thousand dice rolls take about five hours. Of these 1,000 rolls, about 298 of them will be coming out rolls. Of these 298 coming out rolls, eight or nine of them should be 12's. These eight or nine coming out 12's are the key to the whole proposition.

The casino does not let us win, and we don't lose either, if we are betting don't pass and a 12 is rolled on the coming out roll. What we are going to do is make the casino pay us many times more than the cost of these 12's to our don't pass bets.

Casinos know that a person is inclined to be more generous in parting with his bankroll at a crap table after imbibing a few drinks than while cold sober. Because of this smart but simple observation, casinos are incredibly generous with supplying patrons with free drinks. Because most customers double their losses in return for a few drinks, free liquor equals good business.

To qualify for free booze, the customer obviously must be engaged in gambling. He must also be alert and order his drinks when the waitress walks by. It makes no difference to the waitress how much our hero is betting, only that he is betting.

Here's the free-drinks formula: Our enterprising gambler bets both pass and don't pass on the coming out rolls. The only time that he can lose is when a 12 is thrown on the coming out roll. Considering that only eight or nine 12's will be thrown on coming out rolls during five hours, regardless what direction the dice have been taking, he should be able to consume a much greater dollar value in drinks than the cost of a few 12's!

Obviously, if one person attempted this scheme by betting both pass and don't pass, the dealers would spot the ploy and probably feel justified in stopping the flow of freebies. To overcome this obstacle, our player should share this opportunity for free drinks with a friend. This friend should stand at the opposite end of the table and bet opposite what his friend does. In this way the free liquor flow to these two sports can be doubled for the same cost of 12's, which figures to be about four and a half 12's per lush for each five hours of guzzling.

To carry this further, a large group could engage in occupying these two positions by inconspicuously joining and un-joining the table at different locations while keeping only two opposing betting stations operating. Occasionally, simultaneous bets could be made on come and don't come, and at times the betting partners could reverse their roles to make themselves look legitimate while guzzling their free drinks.

If casinos feel justified and honorable by contributing free drinks to their customers to demoralize them and hopefully lower their resistances to foolish bets, they surely should not complain if some customers counter by lowering drink prices with crap-table 12's.

 **GLOSSARY**

**Any Craps:**
A bet that the next roll will be a 2, 3, or 12.

**Any Seven:**
A bet that the next roll will be a 7.

**Back Line:**
Refers to the don't pass area.

**Bar the 12:**
A term found in the don't pass and don't come areas which makes the roll of a 12 (in some casinos the 2) a push between the wrong player and the house.

**Big 6, and Big 8:**
A bet that the 6, or the 8, whichever is bet, will be thrown before a 7 is rolled.

**Box Numbers:**
The boxes numbered, 4, 5, 6, 8, 9, and 10, which are used to mark the point, and to mark place, come, and buy bets.

**Center Bets:**
The bets located in the center of the layout.

**Cold Dice:**
A streak of losing rolls for the right bettors. Good for wrong bettors.

**Come Bet:**

A bet that the dice will win, or pass. Works just like a pass bet except that it can only be made after a point is established.

**Come Bet Coming Out Roll:**

When a pass line point is already established, the first roll of the dice after a come bet is placed and before the come point is established.

**Come Point:**

The throw of a 4, 5, 6, 8, 9, or 10 on the come bet coming-out roll becomes the come point number.

**Coming-Out Roll:**

The roll made before any point has been established.

**Coming Out:**

A term to designate that a new come-out roll is about to happen.

**Contract Bet:**

A bet that, once placed, cannot be removed until a conclusion to it has been reached.

**Correct Odds:**

The mathematical likelihood that a bet will be a winner, expressed in odds.

**Crap Out:**

The roll of a 2, 3, or 12 on a coming-out roll, an automatic loser for pass line bettors.

**Craps:**

Term used to denote a 2, 3, or 12. Also the name of the game.

**Craps-Eleven:**

A one roll bet combining the Any Craps and 11.

**Dealer:**

The casino employee who works directly with the player and who handles all monetary transactions and bets.

**Dice:**

The two six-sided cubes, numbered one to six, that are used to play craps.

**Don't Come Bet:**

A bet made against the dice. The bet works just like the don't pass except that it can only be made after a point is established.

**Don't Pass:**

A bet made before a point is established, on the coming-out roll only, that the dice will lose.

**Don't Pass Bet Decision:**

A don't pass bet that gets completed as either a winning or losing bet.

**Double Odds Bet:**

A free-odds bet that allows the player to bet double his line wager as a right bettor, and double the line payoff as a wrong bettor.

**Down:**

An instruction for a dealer to pick up place bets from the numbers and return them to the player.

**Easy, Easy Way:**

The throw of a 4, 6, 8, or 10 other than as a pair, such as a 1 and a 5, *6, the easy way.*

**Edge, House Edge:**

The built-in odds that favor the casino over the player.

**Even-Money:**

The payoff of one dollar for every dollar bet.

**Fade a Bet:**

To put up money and cover a bet.

**Fading Game:**

A private crap game where players, on a rotating basis, shoot the dice and put up money to gamble—and the other players cover the shooter's bets.

**Field Bet:**

A one-roll bet that the next roll of the dice will be a number in the field box—a 2, 3, 4, 9, 10, 11, or 12.

**Field Numbers:**

Numbers rolled that would be winners on the field bet—2, 3, 4, 9, 10, 11 and 12.

**Floorman:**

Casino executive who supervises one or more craps tables.

**Free-Odds Bets:**

A bet made in conjunction with the line, come, and don't come bets, that can only be made after the establishment of a point or come point. The free-odds bet is paid off at the correct odds, with the house having no advantage.

**Front Line:**

Refers to the pass line.

**Hand:**

A sequence of rolls that is completed when the roller throws a 7 after having established a point on a coming out roll. A hand ends only when a 7 is thrown on any roll other than a coming-out roll, a loss on the pass—in other words, a point has been established and now loses ending the hand. As you see, a hand cannot be concluded on just one throw and it can consist of more than one pass bet decision.

**Hardway Bet:**

A sequence bet that the hardway number, the 4, 6, 8, or 10, will come up in doubles before it comes up easy, or before a 7 is thrown.

**Hardway:**

The throw of a 4, 6, 8 or 10 as a pair, such as 3, 3, *6 the hardway*.

**Horn Bet:**

A one roll bet that the next throw will be a 2, 3, 11, or 12.

**Hot Roll:**

An extended succession of winning throws for players betting with the dice. Bad for wrong bettors.

**House:**

A term to denote the casino.

**Inside Numbers:**

The place numbers 5, 6, 8, and 9.

**Insurance:**

A bet made to "protect" another bet—the wager wins on the rolls that the main bet loses on.

**Lay Bet:**

A wager made by wrong bettors that a 7 will show before the point number.

**Layout:**

The felted surface of the craps table where bets are placed, paid off and collected, and where the dice are thrown.

**Lay-up Odds:**

The odds wagered in conjunction with a don't pass or don't come bet.

**Line Bet:**

Refers to a pass or don't pass bet.

**Making a Pass:**

Throwing a natural on the first roll or making a point.

**Odds:**

The number of times an event is likely to happen compared to the number of times the event is likely not to happen. For example, out of the 36 possible combinations on a pair of dice, one of them is 2 (1 + 1) making the odds against a single roll of 2 on the dice 35 to 1.

**Odds Bet:**

See *Free-Odds Bet.*

**Off:**

A designation that a bet is not working on a particular roll.

**On:**

A designation that a bet is working on a particular roll.

**Outside Numbers:**

The place numbers, 4 and 10.

**Over 7:**

A bet that the next roll of the dice will produce a number greater than 7.

**Parlay or Press:**

The increase of a won bet, usually by doubling it.

**Pass, Pass Line:**

A bet made before a point is established, on the coming-out roll only, that the dice will pass, or win.

**Pass Bet Decision:**

A bet on pass that gets completed as either a winning or losing bet.

**Payoff, House Payoff:**

The amount of money the casino pays the player on a winning bet.

**Place Bet:**

A wager that a particular box number, whichever is bet on, the 4, 5, 6, 8, 9, or 10, will be rolled before a 7.

**Point, Point Number:**

The throw of a 4, 5, 6, 8, 9, or 10 on the coming-out roll becomes the point number.

**Probability:**

The ratio of the number of times that an event is likely to happen compared to the whole number of ways of which this particular event is a part. For example, the probability for having two dice add to 2 is 1 out of 36 rolls.

**Proposition Bets:**

See *Center Bets.*

**Return:**

The total amount returned to the bettor after he wins a bet including the sum of the amount he bet plus the amount he won. For example, if you bet $1 on a bet and win $2 more, your return would be $3. (Craps tables sometimes state payoffs with a for, as in "30 for 1," which means that a $1 bet will return $30 (not $31). Since $1 is the bet, the casino is actually paying 29 to 1, not the 30 to 1 they would like you to believe.)

**Return Ratio:**

The ratio of what the total return actually is compared to what it would have been had its true odds been applied to the win. For example, when $30 is returned for a winning bet on 2 when $36 would be the return at the true odds, the return ratio is 83.333% (30 ÷ 36 x 100).

**Right Bettors:**

Players betting that the dice will pass. Pass and come bettors.

**Roll or Throw:**

An individual toss of the dice.

**Roller:**

See *Shooter*.

**Seven-Out:**

The roll of a 7 after a point has been established, a loser for pass line bettors.

**Shooter:**

The player throwing the dice.

**Single Odds:**

A free-odds bet that allows the player to bet equal the pass or come bet as a right bettor, and equal the payoff on a don't pass or don't come bet.

**Standoff:**

A tie, nobody wins. Also called a *Push*.

**Sucker Bets:**

Exotic wagers (that is, bad wagers) with long odds that give the house an exorbitant edge against the player.

**Trap Bet:**

A bet that gives you the chance to increase the rate at which you can lose money.

**Under 7:**

A bet that the next roll of the dice will be a number that is less than 7.

**Unit:**

Bet size used as a standard of measurement.

**Working:**

Designation that a bet is "on," that is, in play.

**Wrong Bettors:**

Don't pass and don't come bettors.

## ATTENTION: CRAPS PLAYERS!

If you like this book, come to our website, and browse our extensive library of titles—we not only have the world's largest selection of craps titles (*more than 20 times* the selection of major chain superstores), but over 3,000 total gaming and gambling titles!

# POWERFUL WINNING POKER SIMULATIONS
## A MUST FOR SERIOUS PLAYERS WITH A COMPUTER!
### IBM compatible CD ROM Win 95, 98, 2000, NT, ME, XP

These incredible full color poker simulations are the best method to improve your game. Computer opponents play like real players. All games let you set the limits and rake and have fully programmable players, stat tracking, and Hand Analyzer for starting hands. Mlke Caro, the world's foremost poker theoretician says, "Amazing... a steal for under $500... get it, it's great." Includes free phone support. "Smart Advisor" gives expert advice for every play!

**1. TURBO TEXAS HOLD'EM FOR WINDOWS - $59.95**. Choose which players, and how many (2-10) you want to play, create loose/tight games, and control check-raising, bluffing, position, sensitivity to pot odds, and more! Also, instant replay, pop-up odds, Professional Advisor keeps track of play statistics. Free bonus: Hold'em Hand Analyzer analyzes all 169 pocket hands in detail and their win rates under any conditions you set. Caro says this "hold'em software is the most powerful ever created." Great product!

**2. TURBO SEVEN-CARD STUD FOR WINDOWS - $59.95**. Create any conditions of play; choose number of players (2-8), bet amounts, fixed or spread limit, bring-in method, tight/loose conditions, position, reaction to board, number of dead cards, and stack deck to create special conditions. Features instant replay. Terrific stat reporting includes analysis of starting cards, 3-D bar charts, and graphs. Play interactively and run high speed simulation to test strategies. Hand Analyzer analyzes starting hands in detail. Wow!

**3. TURBO OMAHA HIGH-LOW SPLIT FOR WINDOWS - $59.95**. Specify any playing conditions; betting limits, number of raises, blind structures, button position, aggressiveness/ passiveness of opponents, number of players (2-10), types of hands dealt, blinds, position, board reaction, and specify flop, turn, and river cards! Choose opponents and use provided point count or create your own. Statistical reporting, instant replay, pop-up odds  high speed simulation to test strategies, amazing Hand Analyzer, and much more!

**4. TURBO OMAHA HIGH FOR WINDOWS - $59.95**. Same features as above, but tailored for Omaha High only. Caro says program is "an electrifying research tool...it can clearly be worth thousands of dollars to any serious player." A must for Omaha High players.

**5. TURBO 7 STUD 8 OR BETTER - $59.95**.  Brand new with all the features you expect from the Wilson Turbo products: the latest artificial intelligence, instant advice and exact odds, play versus 2-7 opponents, enhanced data charts that can be exported or printed, the ability to fold out of turn and immediately go to the next hand, ability to peek at opponents hand, optional warning mode that warns you if a play disagrees with the advisor, and automatic mode that runs up to 50 tests unattended. Tough computer players vary their styles for a great game.

**6. TOURNAMENT TEXAS HOLD'EM - $39.95**
Set-up for tournament practice and play, this realistic simulation pits you against celebrity look-alikes. Tons of options let you control tournament size with 10 to 300 entrants, select limits, ante, rake, blind structures, freezeouts, number of rebuys and competition level of opponents. Pop-up status report shows how you're doing vs. the competition. Save tournaments in progress to play again later. Additional feature allows quick folds on finished hands.

# Win at Blackjack Without Counting Cards!!!

## Multiple Deck 1, 2, 3 Non-Counter - Breakthrough in Blackjack!!!

### BEAT MULTIPLE DECK BLACKJACK WITHOUT COUNTING CARDS!

You heard right! Now, for the **first time ever**, **win** at multiple deck blackjack **without counting cards**! Until I developed the Cardoza Multiple Deck Non-Counter (the 1,2,3 Strategy), I thought it was impossible. Don't be intimidated anymore by four, six or eight deck games—for **you have the advantage**. It doesn't matter how many decks they use, for this easy-to-use and proven strategy keeps you **winning—with the odds**!

### EXCITING STRATEGY—ANYONE CAN WIN! -

We're **excited** about this strategy for it allows anyone at all, against any number of decks, to have the **advantage** over any casino in the world in a multiple deck game. You don't count cards, you don't need a great memory, you don't need to be good at math - you just need to know the **winning secrets** of the 1,2,3 Multiple Deck Non-Counter and use but a **little effort** to win $$$.

### SIMPLE BUT EFFECTIVE! -

Now the answer is here. This strategy is so **simple**, yet so **effective**, you will be amazed. With a **minimum of effort**, this remarkable strategy, which we also call the 1,2,3 (as easy as 1,2,3), allows you to win without studiously following cards. Drink, converse with your fellow players or dealer - they'll never suspect that you can **beat the casino**!

### PERSONAL GUARANTEE -

And you have my personal **guarantee of satisfaction**, 100% money back! This breakthrough strategy is my personal research and is guaranteed to give you the edge! If for any reason you're not satisfied, send back the materials unused within 30 days for a full refund.

### BE A LEISURELY WINNER! -

If you just want to play a **leisurely game** yet have the expectation of winning, the answer is here. Not as powerful as a card counting strategy, but **powerful enough to make you a winner** - with the odds!!!

### EXTRA BONUS! -

Complete listing of all options and variations at blackjack and how they affect the player. ($5.00 Value!)

### EXTRA, EXTRA BONUS!! -

Not really a bonus since we can't sell you the strategy without protecting you against getting barred. The 1,000 word essay, "How to Disguise the Fact That You're an Expert," and the 1,500 word "How Not To Get Barred," are also included free. ($15.00 Value)

To order, send ~~$75~~ $50 (plus postage and handling) by check or money order to:
Cardoza Publishing, P.O. Box 98115, Las Vegas, NV 89193

- - - - - - - - - - - - - - - - - - - - - - - - - - - - -

## $25 OFF! (Only $50 With This Coupon!)

**Yes!** I want to be a winner at blackjack! Please rush me the **Cardoza Multiple Deck Non-Counter** (The **1,2,3 Strategy**). I understand that all the two bonus essays, and the "Options and Variations" Charts all will be included **absolutely free**! Enclosed is a check or money order for $50 (plus postage and handling) made out to:

Cardoza Publishing, P.O. Box 98115, Las Vegas, NV 89193

### MC/Visa/Amex Orders Toll-Free in U.S. & Canada, 1-800-577-WINS

Include $5.00 postage/handling for U.S. orders; $10.00 for Can/Mex; HI/AK and other countries $15.00. Outside U.S., money order payable in U.S. dollars on U.S. bank only.

NAME_____

ADDRESS_____

CITY_____ STATE _____ ZIP _____

**MC/Visa/Amex Orders By Mail**

MC/Visa/Amex # _____ Phone _____

Exp. Date _____ Signature _____

Crap Shooter

### Order Now! 30 Day Money Back Guarantee!

# WIN MONEY AT BLACKJACK! SPECIAL OFFER!
## THE CARDOZA BASE COUNT STRATEGY

**Finally**, a count strategy has been developed which allows the average player to play blackjack like a **pro**! Actually, this strategy isn't new. The Cardoza Base Count Strategy has been used successfully by graduates of the Cardoza School of Blackjack for years. But **now**, for the **first time**, this "million dollar" strategy, which was only available previously to those students attending the school, is available to **you**!

**FREE VACATIONS! A SECOND INCOME?** - You bet! Once you learn this strategy, you will have the skills to **consistently win big money** at blackjack. The longer you play, the more you make. The casino's bankroll is yours for the taking.

**BECOME AN EXPERT IN TWO DAYS** - Why struggle over complicated strategies that aren't as powerful? In just **two days or less**, you can learn the Cardoza Base Count and be among the best blackjack players. Friends will look up to you in awe - for you will be a **big winner** at blackjack.

**BEAT ANY SINGLE OR MULTIPLE DECK GAME** - We show you how, with just a **little effort**, you can effectively beat any single or multiple deck game. You'll learn how to count cards, how to use advanced betting and playing strategies, how to make money on insurance bets, and much more in this 6,000 word, chart-filled strategy package.

**SIMPLE TO USE, EASY TO MASTER** - **You too can win!** The **power** of the Cardoza Base Count strategy is not only in its **computer-proven** winning results but also in its **simplicity**. Many beginners who thought card counting was too difficult have given the Cardoza Base Count the acid test - they have **won consistently** in casinos around the world. The Cardoza Base Count strategy is designed so that **any player** can win under practical casino conditions. **No need** for a mathematical mind or photographic memory. **No need** to be bogged down by calculations. Keep **only one number** in your head at any time. The casinos will never suspect that you're a counter.

**DOUBLE BONUS!!** - **Rush** your order in **now**, for we're also including, **absolutely free**, the 1,000 and 1,500 word essays, "How to Disguise the Fact that You're an Expert", and "How Not to Get Barred". Among other **inside information** contained here, you'll learn about the psychology of the pit bosses, how they spot counters, how to project a losing image, role playing, and other skills to maximize your profit potential.

As an **introductory offer to readers of this book**, the Cardoza Base Count Strategy, which has netted graduates of the Cardoza School of Blackjack **substantial sums** of **money**, is offered here for **only** $50!

To order, send $50 by check or money order to:

Cardoza Publishing, P.O. Box 98115, Las Vegas, NV 89193

---

# WIN MONEY PLAYING BLACKJACK!
## MAIL THIS COUPON NOW!

**Yes**, I want to **win big money** at blackjack. Please **rush** me the Cardoza Base Count Strategy. I understand that the Double Bonus essays are included **absolutely free**. Enclosed is a check or money order for $50 (plus postage and handling) made out to:

Cardoza Publishing, P.O. Box 98115, Las Vegas, NV 89193
### Call Toll-Free in U.S. & Canada, 1-800-577-WINS

Include $5.00 postage/handling for U.S. orders; $10.00 for Can/Mex; HI/AK and other countries $15.00. Outside U.S., money order payable in U.S. dollars on U.S. bank only.

NAME_____

ADDRESS_____

CITY _____ STATE _____ ZIP _____
Crap Shooter

### Order Now to Win! 30 Day Money Back Guarantee!

# CARDOZA SCHOOL OF BLACKJACK
## - Home Instruction Course - $200 OFF! -

**At last**, after years of secrecy, the **previously unreleased** lesson plans, strategies and playing tactics formerly available only to members of the Cardoza School of Blackjack are now available to the general public - and at substantial savings. **Now**, you can **learn at home,** and at your own convenience. Like the full course given at the school, the home instruction course goes **step-by-ste**p over the winning concepts. We'll take you from layman to **pro.**

**MASTER BLACKJACK** - Learn what it takes to be a **master player**. Be a **powerhouse**, play with confidence, impunity, and **with the odds** on your side. Learn to be a **big winner** at blackjack.

**MAXIMIZE WINNING SESSIONS** - You'll learn how to take a good winning session and make a **blockbuster** out of it, but just as important, you'll learn to cut your losses. Learn exactly when to end a session. We cover everything from the psychological and emotional aspects of play to altered playing conditions (through the **eye of profitability**) to protection of big wins. The advice here could be worth **hundreds (or thousands) of dollars** in one session alone. Take our guidelines seriously.

**ADVANCED STRATEGIES** - You'll learn the latest in advanced winning strategies. Learn about the **ten-factor**, the **ace-factor**, the effects of rules variations, how to protect against dealer blackjacks, the winning strategies for single and multiple deck games and how each affects you; the **true count**, the multiple deck true count variations, and much, much more. And, of course, you'll receive the full Cardoza Base Count Strategy package.

**$200 OFF - LIMITED OFFER** - The Cardoza School of Blackjack home instruction course, retailed at $295 (or $895 if taken at the school) is available here for just $95.

**DOUBLE BONUS!** - **Rush** your order in **now**, for we're also including, **absolutely free**, the 1,000 and 1,500 word essays, "How to Disguise the Fact that You're an Expert", and "How Not to Get Barred". Among other **inside information** contained here, you'll learn about the psychology of the pit bosses, how they spot counters, how to project a losing image, role playing, and other skills to maximize your profit potential.

To order, send $95 (plus postage and handling) by check or money order to:
Cardoza Publishing, P.O. Box 98115, Las Vegas, NV 89193